Clout

the ART and SCIENCE of
INFLUENTIAL WEB CONTENT

COLLEEN JONES

New
Riders

VOICES THAT MATTER™

Clout: The Art and Science of Influential Web Content

Colleen Jones

New Riders
1249 Eighth Street
Berkeley, CA 94710
510/524-2178
510/524-2221 (fax)

Find us on the Web at: www.newriders.com
To report errors, please send a note to errata@peachpit.com
New Riders is an imprint of Peachpit, a division of Pearson Education.
Copyright © 2011 by Content Science, LLC.

Project Editor: Michael J. Nolan
Development Editor: Jeff Riley/Box Twelve Communications
Production Editor: Rebecca Winter
Copyeditor: Gretchen Dykstra
Proofreader: Doug Adrianson
Indexer: Julie Bess
Cover Designer: Mimi Heft
Interior Designer: Kim Scott
Compositor: Danielle Foster

ISBN 13: 978-0-321-73301-6
ISBN 10:   0-321-73301-0

9 8 7 6 5 4 3 2

Printed and bound in the United States of America

FOREWORD

The web is all about action verbs. We click. We search. We navigate. We make choices. Alone among other forms of media, we're the ones who control our experience.

When organizations try to connect with their customers online, one of the first things they always want to know is "how can we get our users to do what we want them to?"

There's an answer to this question, but it requires a change in mindset. Marketers typically want to build awareness for their products, and they try to replicate this broadcast approach on the web. They create static designs that recall print ads, flashy microsites that replicate TV commercials, and email blasts that resemble nothing so much as a street-corner barker, yelling loudly while he tries to press a flyer into your hand.

And then they wonder why users don't do what they want them to.

Organizations that want to connect with users online need to shift their approach from gaining awareness to building influence. Persuading people to behave differently means understanding how to inspire people, motivate them, and gain their trust.

The user experience field might rightfully say: "Influencing user behavior? Why, that's what we do!" And it's true—if you're looking for techniques to prod people into behaving a certain way, your friendly user experience designer can help you. They'll tell you that the way to get users to do what you want them to is to design a sexier landing page, chunk pages so they flow better, and create an eye-catching call to action. Not working well enough? Just A/B test different options until you find the optimal design.

We've lost our influence with users because our obsession with the medium means we've lost our focus on what really matters — the message. We're so focused on form that we've forgotten about substance. It's time to bring attention back to what we want to say, not just how and where we want to say it.

Well, guess what? Long before there even was a web, we knew how to communicate our messages by tailoring them to the needs and expectations of an audience. We knew how to persuade people by appealing to logic or emotion. We knew the art of rhetoric.

Now, "rhetoric" might seem like the province of glad-handing politicians and oily salesmen, bombastic orators trying to convince naive rubes to part with their hard-earned cash. If that's what you're imagining, let me assure you: Colleen Jones is the exact opposite of that stereotype. With clear reasoning and straightforward prose, she'll make the art and science of persuasion accessible to everyone.

In this book, Leen provides a solid framework for thinking about how to influence people's attitudes, behaviors, and decisions online. She draws on decades of research in rhetoric and technical communication, outlining a few key principles that can help any organization be more persuasive on the web.

This book will offer practical advice to anyone who wants to influence behavior or decision-making using the web. But don't expect to find just tips and tricks—Leen offers a holistic approach to content strategy that will tie all your communication efforts together, including your website, social media, search, and even customer service.

Wondering how to get your users to do what you want them to? You need *Clout*.

—*Karen McGrane, Managing Partner, Bond Art + Science*

ACKNOWLEDGMENTS

I thought writing a book would be hard. I was wrong. Writing a book is *very* hard. *Clout* wouldn't be in your hands without the help of these outstanding people.

I can't thank Michael Nolan, Jeff Riley, and the delightful team at New Riders enough for their wisdom, talent, and collaboration.

Many thanks to the 130+ people in the content strategy and user experience communities around the world who responded to my survey about *Clout*. Your thoughts helped shape its direction.

Kristina Halvorson tore down barriers to more and better discussion about web content, inspired me to contribute, and shared her smart advice. Thank you!

Karen McGrane eloquently discusses all aspects of user experience. And, she demonstrates how a technical communication background (also my background) can lead to executive vision. I'm honored that *Clout* begins with her foreword.

I owe special thanks to these thought leaders for contributing quotes, examples, or case studies:

- Conal Byrne and Tracy V. Wilson, HowStuffWorks.com
- David Almacy, Edelman
- John Muehlbauer, InterContinental Hotels Group
- Bert DuMars and Susan Wassel, Newell Rubbermaid
- Kelly Holton, Centers for Disease Control and Prevention
- Jonathan Kay, Grasshopper.com
- Jim Coudal, The Deck
- Erin Pettigrew, Gawker Media
- Alan Segal, Cox Media Group
- Scott Thomas, Simple Scott and BarackObama.org
- Alan Beychok and Trish Tobin, FootSmart.com
- Tim Jones, North Carolina State University

I'm also grateful to Jeffrey MacIntyre, Rachel Lovinger, BJ Fogg, Jeffrey Zeldman, Erin Kissane, Jeff Chasin, Robert Krause, Shelly Bowen, Rahel Bailie, Sally Bagshaw, Dechay Watts, and Debbie Williams for contributing their insights, connections, or examples.

And I thank Carolyn Wood of *A List Apart* for nudging me to write "Words That Zing," which laid groundwork for this book. I also thank Pabini Gabriel-Petit of *UXmatters* for supporting my past column about content.

I'm indebted to Toni Pashley for holding me accountable. (Margaritas are motivating!) And thanks to Margot Bloomstein, Jonathan Kahn, Destry Wion, Kevin O'Connor, Mike Schinkel, Jeff Hilimire, Chris Moritz, and David Forbes for their enthusiasm early on.

Finally, I extend a heartfelt thanks to Kim Ware for her assistance with editing as well as creating and managing the hundreds of figures. Thanks also to Laura Nolte for helping me spread the news about this book.

ABOUT THE AUTHOR

Colleen Jones has led interactive strategy for Fortune 500 companies such as InterContinental Hotels Group and Cingular Wireless (now AT&T) as well as for Centers for Disease Control and Prevention, the most trusted government agency in the United States. As the principal of Content Science, Colleen consults with executives and practitioners about making their web content more influential. Colleen is a veteran of the interactive industry, a participant in the first ever Content Strategy Consortium, and the founder of Atlanta Content Strategy. She has spoken about the value of compelling web content at conferences everywhere from Phoenix to Paris. Please send her any feedback at colleen@content-science.com.

CONTENTS

INTRODUCTION

• •

CONGRATULATIONS FOR TAKING a big step toward better web content. I'm thrilled to be your guide on a journey to make your content influence results. But, first, let me orient you.

HOW DID *CLOUT* COME ABOUT?

This book is a labor of love—my love for content strategy, persuasion, and positive change. Because people use the web now more than ever to make decisions, everyone from big brands to small businesses to individuals has the opportunity to *influence* those decisions. My goal is to help you make the most of that opportunity.

I also intend this book to solve problems I see again and again in the interactive industry, such as

- Targeting customers with manipulative tricks.
- Publishing *more* instead of *better* web content.
- Spending too much time and money on search engine optimization (SEO) snake oil or misguided advertising.
- Getting on social networks without any thought about supporting content.
- Publishing content that doesn't get results.

WHY PRINCIPLES?

Most of this book explains principles of influence from rhetoric and psychology. Why not start with tactics instead? The reason is simple: **Learning and practicing principles is quicker in the long run.**

Understanding these principles takes time up front, but then you can apply them to any business or project. That's much faster than throwing a bunch of tactics out on the web and inferring why they worked (or, more likely, why they *didn't* work). As Ralph Waldo Emerson has said,

> *"The man who grasps principles can successfully select his own methods. The man who tries methods, ignoring principles, is sure to have trouble."*

I want you to have success, not trouble.

WHO SHOULD READ *CLOUT*—AND HOW?

While anyone on the web can benefit from this book, I've written it with these audiences in mind.

CONTENT, CREATIVE, AND BRAND STRATEGISTS

You love web content and plan for it strategically. Here's how to use this book:

- Make the case for spending time and money on content with familiar and not-so-familiar arguments in chapters 1 and 2.
- Learn the art and science of influence in chapters 3 through 5.
- Jump-start your planning with chapters 6 and 7.
- Evaluate your content efforts with the help of chapters 8–10.
- Consider the call to our industry in chapter 11.

EXECUTIVES

You have a 10,000-foot view of what's happening with your business on the web. Here's how to use this book:

- Read chapters 1, 2, and 11 to understand why influential content is *mission critical*.
- If your industry is health, learn why content is a huge opportunity for you in chapter 11.
- Scan the rest for
  - Insight into the time and effort needed to plan and evaluate influential content.
  - Examples and case studies from big brands such as IHG, CDC, Rubbermaid, Sharpie, HowStuffWorks.com, and more.

WEB WRITERS AND CONTENT CREATORS

You love crafting quality content, whether it's words, photos, podcasts, music, or video. Here's how to use this book:

- Get inspiration for content ideas in chapters 3 through 5.
- Plan content using patterns of influence in chapter 6.
- Gain insight into evaluating content from chapters 8–10.

INTERACTIVE MARKETERS AND PR SPECIALISTS

You're finding more and more that content makes or breaks your campaigns. And, beyond campaigns, you now have to plan for *entire customer relationships*. Here's how to use this book:

- Make the case for spending time and money on content with chapters 1 and 2.
- Learn the art and science of influence in chapters 3 through 5.
- Jump-start your planning with chapters 6 and 7.
- Learn the value of qualitative evaluation from chapters 8–10.
- Consider the call to improve the interactive industry in chapter 11.

SMALL BUSINESS OWNERS

For many of you, the web is your biggest—sometimes only—presence in the world. You know it's important, but you get conflicting advice about what to do. Here's how to use this book:

- Learn why influential content is a valuable investment from chapters 1 and 2.

- Get inspiration for content ideas in chapters 3 through 5.

- Plan content with chapters 6 and 7, then get help with evaluating in chapters 8–10.

NONPROFITS AND PEOPLE WHO DO GOOD

You're realizing the power of the web to move your cause forward. Here's how to use this book:

- Make the case for funding content with chapters 1 and 2.

- Learn the art and science of influence in chapters 3 through 5.

- Plan content with help from chapters 6 and 7.

- Evaluate your content efforts with the help of chapters 8–10.

With first things covered, you're ready to start the journey toward clout.

THE
CROSSROADS

· ·

When it comes to attaining results on the web, we face two ways not equally fair. One way follows the same old road to give us the same old results. The other way is harder and higher—but promises remarkable results. *Which way will you choose?*

1 SAME ROAD, SAME (LACK OF) RESULTS

• •

Expecting old solutions to bring new outcomes always disappoints.

INSANITY: DOING THE SAME THING OVER AND OVER
AGAIN AND EXPECTING DIFFERENT RESULTS.
—Albert Einstein

Results. From improving health to drawing advertisers to selling products, everyone wants results. But, on the web, many of us aren't getting them. We face an important choice.

For more than 13 years, I've watched the interactive industry try these same approaches again and again, hoping for a different result.

PUSHY TRICKS AND SMALL TWEAKS

Think about conversions, a critical result. To make a sale or get a lead, many websites use persuasion like a pushy salesperson, aiming high-pressure ploys at people as if they're stupid targets. One trick I love to hate is the countdown timer. Every tick of the timer tries to rush me into signing up.

Such tricks act like prods to push people along. Do they get results?

Many consultants say we should expect 2 to 3 percent of people who visit websites to convert (buy a product, for example). In fact, the global conversion rate as noted by the Fireclick Index has hovered around 2 to 4 percent since 2003.[1] Let's look at online retail, an industry that depends heavily on conversions. Most online retailers don't exceed 10 percent in their conversion rates.[2] In other words, at least 90 percent of visitors to most online retail websites do not buy. Even if you consider that not everyone who visits a retail website intends to buy, these rates are low.

How can we improve? Ever since testing tools—such as Google Website Optimizer in 2006—came on the scene, many consultants tell us testing and optimizing are the answer. We're encouraged to tweak the text, buttons, and pictures on our websites and landing pages until conversion rates rise. (That's sometimes where manipulative tricks come in, too.) We've had years to experiment. If tricks and tweaks worked so well, the global conversion rate would have improved, if not skyrocketed, by now.

Should you stop testing or stop optimizing? No. But that shouldn't be all you do. Tricks and tweaks, by themselves, are not enough to get meaningful results.

OVERPROMISED TECHNOLOGY

No IT product, feature, or widget *alone* will give you results. I don't care what the smiley vendor with the slick demo and the free drinks says! Tom Davenport, an industry analyst and author, has pointed out the limits of technology.

"The important point, however, is that we need more naysayers in the IT field... Most products don't work as advertised or very well in general, and even more are unworthy of the hype that surrounds them."[3]

Time and again, I've watched companies—especially big ones—look to an IT product as the quick pill to cure all ills. Time and again, I've watched those companies try to launch that IT product through a doomed project. In fact, reports of research by Standish Group, Dynamic Markets Limited, and others suggest most IT projects fail.[4, 5] Those projects remind me a lot of this Dilbert cartoon (**Figure 1.1**).

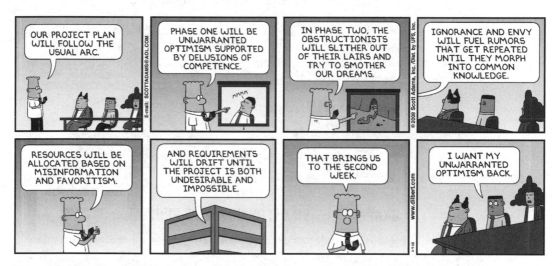

Figure 1.1: Many IT projects start with unrealistic expectations and end in disappointment.

SEO SNAKE OIL

A cousin of overpromised technology, SEO snake oil is the promise of high search engine rankings with little effort. Who sells it? Slippery SEO consultants who take advantage of the fact that search engine formulas aren't public. They're held more sacred than your grandmother's secret recipe. Those formulas also change regularly. So, no one—including no consultant—knows *exactly* what ranks your website. The snake oil consultants "guarantee" rankings and make dubious recommendations. One of my favorites is to post lots of articles crammed with keywords. The result often is gibberish that humans can't understand. And, these consultants insist the effort is worth spending a chunk of change.

Now, there is legitimate SEO work done by good SEO consultants. They experiment with different variables and observe what affects your search engine rankings. Mostly, good web design and content go a long way toward good SEO. I don't mean you should throw out SEO concerns.

SEO snake oil, however, leads people to spend money on being found (which often doesn't work) at the expense of making their website *worth finding*. If your website is mired in meaningless articles "for SEO purposes," you're not going to get results.

DESIGN ALONE

An eye-catching and easy-to-use website is good. But, is that all you need for results?

GRAPHIC DESIGN HELPS BUT ISN'T ENOUGH

Good graphic design gives people a fantastic first impression so they don't leave your website right away. It also helps set your style. Those benefits are valuable but, by themselves, don't sustain results for the long term. How many beautiful websites have you visited once and then forgotten? Oh, wait, you probably don't remember.

USABILITY AND INTERACTION ARE IMPORTANT—BUT YOU NEED MORE

Deeper design, such as whether a website has a user-friendly interface, is important. If people can't interact well with your website, you have a major problem. Usability is even a common courtesy that will help your reputation.[6] But, this deeper design does not fully address the substance of most websites—content.

Persuasive Design: A Little Knowledge Is a Dangerous Thing

Persuasive design is the effort to apply persuasion research to design, especially graphic and interaction design. Persuasive design has potential to help results. (For a practical introduction, see *Neuro Web Design*.) The problems?

1. Practitioners don't get enough time to learn persuasion deeply enough to apply it well. The result often is pushy tricks.

2. Persuasive design does not address content—the substance of most websites.

SHORTSIGHTED MARKETING

I used to think getting results online was marketing's job. I changed my mind when I kept running into these problems.

BROADCASTING DOESN'T WORK FOR THE INTERACTIVE WEB

Since the late 1990s, marketing has claimed to adapt to the web. Before then, marketing followed a broadcast model, which treated the company brand as a battleship blasting its message at targets (the customers). Usually, the blasts were campaigns or promotions, which lasted for a few weeks or months.

While marketers still talk about becoming interactive, it largely hasn't happened. A 2010 *Harvard Business Review* article has called for the complete reinvention of marketing and states (emphasis mine):

"To compete in this aggressively interactive environment, companies must shift their focus **from driving transactions** to maximizing customer lifetime value. That means making products and brands subservient **to long-term customer relationships**."[7]

Most marketers I encounter still blast a message at customers rather than plan to interact with customers for the long term.

WEB ADS ARE ANYTHING BUT INFLUENTIAL

Banner ads. Pop-up windows. Distracting videos. Online ads are so bad, they're infamous. It's easy to blame the designers. But, the real problem is with the advertising system. As Karen McGrane, president of Bond Art + Science and a researcher of online advertising, pointed out:

"There are any number of reasons that web ads are terrible, but most of them sit far upstream from the beleaguered agency art director asked to churn out banner ads each week."[8]

McGrane explains that advertisers spend too little money on ads through a system with too many creative constraints. She also observes that the ads try to raise awareness of a message rather than persuade.

I could go on, and I bet you could add to this list of tried-and-untrue solutions.

It's time to stop driving ourselves crazy. The only way to different results is a different road. I'm convinced that different road is building clout through influential content.

SUMMARY

As you work for results on the web, beware of misleading shortcuts. Avoid the lure of pushy tricks, a magical IT product, SEO snake oil, design without substance, and outdated marketing techniques. Those shortcuts are really dead ends. Instead, take a harder but more rewarding road—the road to influential content.

REFERENCES

1 Web Analytics Benchmark at index.fireclick.com/

2 Top 10 Online Retailers by Conversion Rate (June 2007–March 2010) at www.marketingcharts.com

3 In Praise of IT Naysayers at http://blogs.hbr.org/davenport/2007/07/in_praise_of_it_naysayers.html

4 Recession Causes Rising IT Project Failure Rates at www.cio.com/article/495306/Recession_Causes_Rising_IT_Project_Failure_Rates

5 Two Reasons Why IT Projects Continue to Fail at advice.cio.com/remi/two_reasons_why_it_projects_continue_to_fail

6 Steve Krug, Don't Make Me Think! (New Riders, 2005)

7 Rethinking Marketing at http://hbr.org/2010/01/rethinking-marketing/ar/1

8 Why Web Ads Suck at http://karenmcgrane.com/2009/05/22/why-web-ads-suck/

2 A HARDER BUT HIGHER ROAD

· ·

The way to get results online is clout—influence or pull. Achieving clout demands new thinking and a new focus on web content.

THE GREATEST ABILITY IN BUSINESS IS TO GET ALONG WITH OTHERS AND TO INFLUENCE THEIR ACTIONS.

—John Hancock

The way to get results on the web, no matter your goal, is to achieve *clout*.

A NEW WAY OF THINKING

Clout is influence or pull. On the web, clout allows you (or your organization) to attract the right people and, at the right time, change what they think or do. Clout isn't achieved with only a quick trick, a personalization feature, a sexy design, a tweet, or a campaign blast. Rather, clout is the outcome of publishing influential web content during lasting relationships with people.

This thinking demands sophistication and substance. Crass tactics that the interactive industry often calls persuasion or influence simply will not do, as I explained in Chapter 1. How does our thinking need to change? **Table 2.1** summarizes the biggest shifts we need, and the rest of this book will explain them.

Table 2.1: Changes in Thinking to Achieve Clout

OLD THINKING	NEW THINKING
Target people	Attract people
Plan for campaigns	Plan for entire customer relationships
Tell, or talk, the message	Tell and show, or walk, the message
Blast the message repeatedly	Reveal facets of the message
Force or trick	Nudge
Detached	Contextual
Action only	Attitude and action

Just as important, this new way of thinking requires a new focus on content.

WEB CONTENT IS THE KEY TO CLOUT

Many people are on the web, and they need content to help them make decisions. That's a big opportunity to influence. Let's consider it in more detail.

THE WEB IS WHERE PEOPLE ARE

Most people, from teens to seniors, are online. For example, in the United States 74 percent of adults and 93 percent of teens use the Internet (**Figure 2.1**).[1]

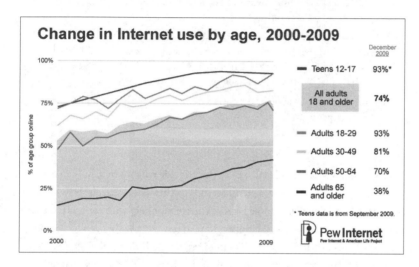

Figure 2.1: Most teens and adults in the United States are online.

Knowing where people are is half the battle in business. As billionaire entrepreneur Ray Kroc has noted, "The two most important requirements for major success are: first, being in the right place at the right time, and second, doing something about it."

Now is the time for organizations large and small to be on the web. What should you do about it? Give people what they want.

CONTENT IS WHAT PEOPLE WANT

Content is the stuff—text, data, graphics, video, and audio—that people want on the web.[2] People spend lots of time reading, viewing, or listening to content online. People share and comment on content over social networking. And, new studies show that many other people never share or comment but they *do* pay attention to what others do.[3] It's as if they read, not converse, over social networks.

Blasting the Myth That People Don't Read

. . . .

"Just post it—no one will read it anyway."

If anyone has said that to you as an excuse not to spend time on web content—especially text—then take heart. Research is on your side. The Poynter EyeTrack07 study shows that people actually read more deeply online than offline. (For an insightful discussion of the study, see "Myth: People Read Less Online" by Erin Kissane at http://incisive.nu/2010/myth-people-read-less-online/.)

Where did this myth come from? One source is Jakob Nielsen's study "Concise, SCANNABLE, and Objective: How to Write for the Web." For my take on problems with this study, see my blog post "How Users Read on the Web Redux" at http://www.leenjones.com/2009/06/how-users-read/.

In short, people *do* read web content, so web content is a huge opportunity to influence people.

Content is also what people turn to as they decide what to buy, how to care for their health, how to vote, and more, as Pew Internet research shows again and again.[4, 5, 6] Likewise, people turn to the web for help with topics that scare or embarrass them. (For a fascinating look at how we use the web to decide, read Bill Tancer's *Click: What Millions of People Are Doing Online and Why It Matters*.) In short, people look to web content now more than ever for help with their decisions. Will *your* web content shape those decisions?

CONTENT CAN INFLUENCE LIKE PEOPLE CAN INFLUENCE

With or without social networking, web content is a public conversation between your company's people and your users. Your content speaks for your organization. Your content can even take on a personality through its voice or tone. If your content speaks well, it grows a relationship between your company and your customers or users. Then, in the context of that relationship, your content can persuade.

I find web content persuades best when it acts like a trusted advisor or consultant—what academics call a "social actor."[7] In your industry, you might find inspiration from a person or role that tends to be the advisor to your customers offline. **Figure 2.2** shows a summary of inspiration I've found in different industries. Does *your* web content act and sound like a trusted advisor?

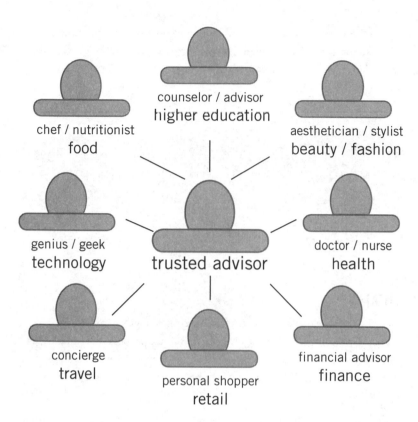

chef / nutritionist
food

counselor / advisor
higher education

aesthetician / stylist
beauty / fashion

genius / geek
technology

trusted advisor

doctor / nurse
health

concierge
travel

personal shopper
retail

financial advisor
finance

Figure 2.2:
Draw inspiration for your
web content from your
industry's trusted advisor.

CONTENT IS EVERYWHERE

It's easier than ever for people to access web content. You can deliver
content through all kinds of tools and channels. You have the power to give
people the right content for their situation. That's like having the power to
say the right thing in the right place at the right time. If content is everywhere, so is your opportunity to influence. Are you making the most of it?

BUT, WEB CONTENT IS HARD

"*Of course* we'll have the right content."

That's how some of my clients first responded when I said the best way to
influence people is web content. Such clients assume that the right content
will find its way to their website. Dangerous assumption!

Content does not magically appear from fairy dust—no matter how hard you wish for it. You have to plan. You also have to think about content strategy and quality before you can even hope for influence (**Figure 2.3**).

Figure 2.3: Content strategy and quality are linked to content influence.

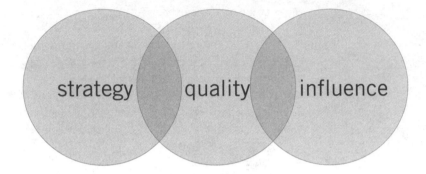

STRATEGY

Content strategy plans for creating, delivering, and governing quality content.[8] Forming a content strategy is an intense process. Fortunately, a guide is available—*Content Strategy for the Web* by Kristina Halvorson. I also recommend finding an experienced content strategist to advise you along the way.

Critical to content strategy is deciding what your goals are and how content will help you achieve them. At a minimum, those decisions require

- An understanding of your organization's goals
- An assessment of whether the content you have meets those goals
- A decision as to what content to throw out, update, repurpose, or add

QUALITY

As you carry out your strategy, you will improve the quality of your web content. You can tell when your content starts to have these characteristics (**Table 2.2**).

Table 2.2: Characteristics of Quality Content

CHARACTERISTIC	DESCRIPTION
Usable and Findable	The content is easy to find, access, and read.
Clear and Accurate	The content is understandable, organized cohesively, and correct.
Complete	The content meets customer needs with the right amount of content for the situation.
Consistent	The content across the website or interactive experience is similar in style, tone, and approach.
Useful and Relevant	The content meets user and business goals. It is timely and pertinent.

Creating quality content is no less intense than forming the strategy for it. It's not simply writing articles or posting pictures. You often need elements like these *behind* the scenes.

Excellent Editorial Oversight

Editorial oversight is having real, live humans involved in decisions about your website content. Technology can't make those decisions for you. People have to plan topics, develop your brand's voice and style, and review every bit of content you publish. It's the only way to ensure your content works well for other people.

HowStuffWorks.com, for example, relies on strong editorial guidance. Editor-in-Chief Conal Byrne notes there is "no substitute" for "vetted, edited, reliable, and engaging content."[14]

Flexible Content Structure and Efficient Production

Without getting too technical, well-structured content works for people *and* for technology. When content is structured well in a database or content management system, a website can integrate different types of content and show relevant content more accurately. This flexibility requires understanding and documenting the technical side of content and the relationships between different pieces of content. To boot, a good content structure usually makes your website easier to find through search and more accessible.

For efficient production, deciding whether and how to use a content management system, planning the workflow for publishing different types of content, and identifying ways to repurpose content are just some of the concerns.

Flexibility and efficiency were top of mind when the *New York Times* redesigned *T: The New York Times Style Magazine*. The redesign transformed *T* from a stylized Flash site to a blog-inspired site with daily updates. The new site better integrates content and makes content production faster.

"By integrating the best technologies of NYTimes.com with *T*'s visually arresting images and thought-provoking content by our marquee columnists and contributors, we believe our readers will find the site even more engaging, immersive and useful," said Stefano Tonchi, editor of the magazine.[9]

Denise Warren, SVP and chief advertising officer, The New York Times Media Group, added, "The new site is more reader- and advertiser-friendly, and it is better integrated into search, opening the renowned content of *T* to a broader audience of readers."

Quality Content Books More Hotel Rooms for Holiday Inn

InterContinental Hotels Group (IHG)—an international hotel company with seven brands including InterContinental Hotels and Resorts, Crowne Plaza, Hotel Indigo, Holiday Inn, Holiday Inn Express, Staybridge Suites, and Candlewood Suites—conducted a content experiment with remarkable results. IHG wanted to know whether professional-quality content about their hotel properties would perform better than the regular content, which was created by property owners. In other words, would professional photos and descriptions of a hotel influence customers to book it better than owner-generated photos and descriptions?

IHG created high-quality photos and text for a sample of Holiday Inn hotels. Then, they diverted a segment of www.holidayinn.com visitors to that sample of hotels. Finally, IHG conducted extensive analysis to compare bookings for the sample hotels and the hotels with owner-generated content.

The results were stunning. Hotel properties with the high-quality photos and text outperformed owner-generated photos and text by a statistically significant margin. While IHG cannot release the exact numbers, the results were so impressive that executives kicked off a long-term project to revamp the photos and descriptions for *all* Holiday Inn hotels.

"We were amazed at the impact that better quality content had on online hotel bookings. Our goal is to connect guests with great hotels. We believe that professional photos and descriptions help guests more easily decide whether a property is right for them," says John Muehlbauer, Director, Product Strategy and Planning.

These elements are not easy or cheap, but they're achievable and necessary if you want results. When you improve the quality of your content, you can start influencing through it.

Three useful resources to help you improve the quality of your content include

- *The Web Content Strategist's Bible* by Richard Sheffield
- *Letting Go of the Words* by Ginny Redish
- *The Nimble Report* by Rachel Lovinger

INFLUENCE

Influence? Persuasion? "I'm not a used car salesperson," you might protest. And I wouldn't blame you for your objection. Fortunately, I don't mean the manipulation discussed in pseudoscientific self-help books. I'm talking about the art and science of influencing people through our web content. Sound mysterious? This book removes the mystery by explaining key principles, applying them to web content, and offering models to inspire you. When you can influence, you can get those elusive results.

THE VALUE: RESULTS NOW, LATER, AND BEYOND PRICE

When you strive for clout through influential web content, your organization will benefit in several ways.

BUILDING A GOOD REPUTATION

I've worked with all kinds of organizations: large and small, established and start-up, government and private. I'm convinced every type of organization benefits from, if not *depends on*, a good reputation. Reputation is what other people think about your business's character. That character shows in your web content. When your business or organization's presence is exclusively online, your web content is the *only* place to show your character.

If your web content is of good quality, then you give the impression of good character. For example, a reputation for excellent content grew HowStuff-Works.com from a small website by professor Marshall Brain to a subsidiary of the world's number one nonfiction media company, Discovery Communications.

EARNING LOYALTY—AND SOME SLACK

If you keep up this good reputation for a while, then your business earns people's trust for the long haul. You develop a relationship with people. People like and have interest in what you say. This trust is important when you ask people to buy your product, consider your (or your advertisers') opinion, or act on your recommendation. HowStuffWorks.com, for instance, still turns out quality content day in and day out. The result? Webby awards, ardent fans, and eager advertisers.

This reputation also makes handling small mistakes during a long customer relationship much easier. People who like and trust you are more likely to give you the benefit of the doubt. Fast Company once asked, "Which one are you more likely to cut some slack: Apple or Microsoft?"[10] I bet you answered Apple. So did Fast Company.

Why? Apple has fiercely loyal fans, and content grows the relationships with fans. Blogs and online publications seem to hang on Steve Jobs's every word. The speculation on, reviews of, and comments about Apple products and decisions ripple through the Internet. The online coverage of Macworld (the annual Apple conference) through video, articles, blog posts, and more, is unlike that for any other brand. And, if you criticize Apple online, expect the consequences. For instance, in 2008 Eric Savitz published an article on the Barron's website that reported some negative assessments about Apple. Enraged Apple fans fired back with more than 100 comments, mostly defending the company.[11]

You might have noticed that Apple doesn't create all this content. However, Apple carefully plants the seeds—through events, promotions, and inter-views—that blossom into influential web content.

GETTING AHEAD OF A CRISIS

Business leader Warren Buffett has quipped, "It takes 20 years to build a reputation and five minutes to ruin it. If you think about that, you'll do things differently."

Regularly plan for influential content, and you'll be at least hours ahead in communication when crisis strikes. Any crisis specialist will tell you that hours are precious when news spreads fast and worldwide across social networks. Too many companies scramble for content as catastrophe hits. Take Domino's Pizza, for example. Rogue Domino's employees videotaped themselves violating all kinds of health regulations while preparing food— then posted the video on YouTube. Millions of people saw it. After 48 hours of delay and plunging stock prices, Domino's finally cobbled together a video of the CEO explaining an action plan and then posted statements on a brand new Twitter account.[12]

A crisis is stressful enough without having to muddle through new content approaches, too. If you plan for influential content anyway, you won't have to muddle.

ATTRACTING THE RIGHT PEOPLE

As you grow your reputation online, your website has gravity. It's like a friendly black hole that draws people in. Then, those people draw *more* people toward you because they tell others *about* your content, share links *to* your content, quote your content, and…you get the idea.

Even better, your website will attract not just *any* people but the *right* people. Who are they? They're the people who match your business goals. Attracting these people makes influencing their attitudes and actions *much* easier for you or your advertisers.

Bryan Eisenberg, a respected online marketing expert, has suggested that driving the wrong people to our websites is a big reason conversion rates stay low.[13] Many online marketers try to push lots of people to a website instead of attracting and influencing people who already have some interest.

When I asked HowStuffWorks.com Editor-in-Chief Conal Byrne what the secret to success was, he explained, "It's no secret. We really try to match people's needs and interests with content on our site."[14] As a result, HowStuffWorks steadily draws the right readers and the right advertisers.

WINNING THAT CONVERSION, AFTER ALL

When your content has built your reputation enough to attract the right people, convincing those people to act is a natural next step. You and the people you're trying to reach already have much in common.

You've dated for a while. Now, you want a commitment. At this point, you need to understand well what will help or hinder a person's decision. Then, you can create content that makes the decision easy and desirable. For example, Grasshopper's landing page offers a voicemail service (**Figure 2.4**). Even if you don't know all the persuasive techniques used, you can quickly see that the content explains the benefits and addresses concerns—*without* pushy tricks.

Figure 2.4:
The Grasshopper landing page presents content that helps people decide.

If you know how to offer the right content for people deciding whether to convert, more people will decide in your favor.

HELPING PEOPLE DECIDE—FOR THE BETTER

Your goal might *not* be entirely commercial. You might want to encourage decisions that make us better people and the world a better place. You might want to help people choose what is best for them and their loved ones. Influential content will help you gently direct people in those choices. For example, the Livestrong Foundation produces an entire website (www.livestrong.com) with articles, videos, tools, and more to help people adopt and stick to a healthy lifestyle.

IF CONTENT IS YOUR LABOR OF LOVE

Consider how you will finance producing quality, influential content—advertising, paid subscriptions, donations, cost savings from other types of marketing? (See the Strategy section in this chapter.)

Don't underestimate the time and resources it takes. Start small, and then grow. Marketing expert Seth Godin cautions, "Keep your overhead low and don't quit your day job until your idea can absorb your time."

The funny thing is that helping people make better decisions is somehow linked to better business (or better funding, if you are a government agency or nonprofit). Take these examples from retail, public health, and consulting (**Table 2.3**).

Table 2.3: Examples of Influencing Decisions with Content

WHO	INFLUENCES DECISIONS ABOUT	USING THIS CONTENT	ENJOYING THIS BENEFIT
Zappos	Happiness	Quotes, comments, and conversations	Bought for estimated $847 million
Centers for Disease Control and Prevention (CDC)	Public health	Articles, podcasts, data	Most trusted U.S. govt. agency
Seth Godin	Change	Blogs and books	Best-selling author and A-list speaker

For Zappos, content such as large product pictures helped customers select shoes and other merchandise. Content also demonstrated Zappos's quirky culture of happiness—and consequently its competitive edge. For the Centers for Disease Control and Prevention (CDC), content shows its public health expertise and responsiveness to crises. For Seth Godin, content articulates his different way of thinking about and doing business.

All of these examples are win-wins. The people who were influenced made better decisions related to happiness, health, and business. The people who did the influencing benefitted in ways so valuable, they are difficult to price. And, all of these situations owe much of their success to influential content.

SUMMARY

The same road with the same middling results or a harder road with potential for extraordinary results—the choice is yours. To try the climb to clout, meet me at the next chapter.

REFERENCES

1 Change in internet access by age group, 2004–2009 at http://www.pewinternet.org/Infographics/2010/Internet-acess-by-age-group-over-time.aspx

2 Kristina Halvorson, *Content Strategy for the Web* (New Riders Press, 2009)

3 Social Media: The Next Great Gateway for Content Discovery? at http://blog.nielsen.com/nielsenwire/online_mobile/social-media-the-next-great-gateway-for-content-discovery/

4 (Pew Internet Studies about deciding) Online shopping. Pew Internet and American Life Project at http://www.pewinternet.org/Reports/2008/Online-Shopping.aspx

5 The social life of health information. Pew Internet and American Life Project at http://www.pewinternet.org/Reports/2009/8-The-Social-Life-of-Health-Information.aspx

6 The Internet's role in campaign 2008. Pew Internet and American Life Project at http://pewinternet.org/Press-Releases/2009/The-Internets-Role-in-Campaign-2008.aspx

7 BJ Fogg, *Persuasive Technology* (Morgan Kaufmann, 2002)

8 Kristina Halvorson, *Content Strategy for the Web* (New Riders Press, 2009)

9 NYT Style Magazine T gets redesign at http://www.designtaxi.com/news/29809/NYT-Style-Magazine-T-Gets-Redesign/www.nytimes.com/tmagazine

10 Innovation: Customers Have Conversations with Brands that Have Good REPUTATIONS at www.fastcompany.com/blog/fast-company-staff/fast-company-blog/innovation-customers-have-conversations-brands-have-good--0

11 Apple Hits Lowest Level Since June; New iPhone Worries at http://blogs.barrons.com/techtraderdaily/2008/02/22/apple-hits-lowest-level-since-june-new-iphone-worries/

12 Video Prank at Domino's Taints Brand at http://www.nytimes.com/2009/04/16/business/media/16dominos.html

13 The Average Conversion Rate: Is It a Myth? at http://www.clickz.com/3628276

14 How Content Works at HowStuffWorks: Make It Matter, Says Editor-in-Chief at http://www.leenjones.com/2008/09/how-content-works-at-howstuffworks-make-it-matter-says-editor-in-chief/

THE PRINCIPLES

Clout begins and ends with understanding context, or the situation. To make your content resonate in any context, learn principles from the ancient art of rhetoric and the modern science of psychology.

3 CONTEXT: WHERE CLOUT BEGINS AND ENDS

• •

We can't influence what we don't understand. Discovering context is hard, but the more you do it, the easier it gets—and the faster you can plan influential content.

FOR ME, CONTEXT IS THE KEY—FROM THAT COMES
THE UNDERSTANDING OF EVERYTHING.

—Kenneth Noland, artist

Context is the situation, or set of circumstances, that surrounds your web content.

For a quick example of context, consider Grasshopper again. This website offers a voicemail service for entrepreneurs. The web content has to *sell* the service to new customers and *support* current customers. The web content is the virtual glue that binds Grasshopper to its entrepreneurial customers—throughout their entire relationship.

I can't emphasize enough that context is important to making your web content influential. Context is the number one principle of clout. **The faster and better you understand context, the faster and better you can influence it through content.**

THE ELEMENTS OF CONTEXT

If context sounds big, that's because it is. But, you can get a handy understanding of context by focusing on a few important elements. In this book, I focus on elements of context that help you influence. Those elements are the result (or goal), users (or customers), the brand, the timing, and the forum or channel (**Figure 3.1**).

Figure 3.1: The elements of context for influential content.

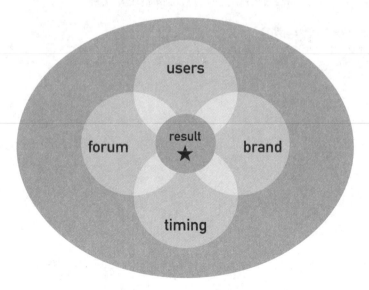

Let's take a closer look at each element, starting with the result you want.

RESULT

What are you trying to do? To accomplish that, do you need to influence what people think, what they do, or both? In my experience, the answer usually is both (**Figure 3.2**).

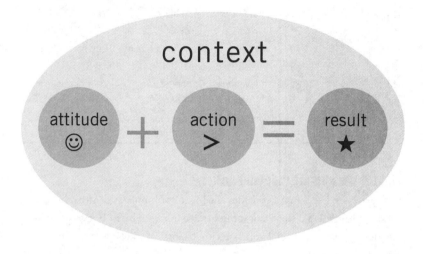

Figure 3.2: Think about whether influencing attitude, action, or both will bring the result you want.

In the case of Grasshopper, one desired result is to get more entrepreneurs to subscribe to its voicemail service. What attitudes and actions help achieve this result? Well, entrepreneurs need to have a good *attitude* toward Grasshopper and its service. For example, entrepreneurs need to find Grasshopper likable and its service trustworthy. And, entrepreneurs need to *act*—to sign up for the service successfully.

Now, your goal might be completely different from Grasshopper's. To jump-start your thinking, **Table 3.1** lists several website goals and, for each, a simple example of a relevant attitude and action.

Table 3.1: Example Results, Attitudes, and Actions in Different Industries

IN THIS INDUSTRY	THIS RESULT	REQUIRES THIS USER ATTITUDE...	AND THIS USER ACTION
Hotel	Sell more hotel rooms	Trust in hotel quality	Book hotel room
Health	Prevent spread of STDs	Personal responsibility	Get an STD test
Retail	Sell expensive clothes	Value high quality	Buy posh dress
Media	Raise ad revenue	Openness to relevant ads	View or click on ad
Higher Education	Enroll excellent students	Respect for reputation	Apply to school

What Makes Up Attitude and Action?

Let's go a step deeper and consider the basic components of attitude and action (**Figure 3.3**). These components are inspired by BJ Fogg's persuasive design research, social construction theory, marketing research, and my practical experience.

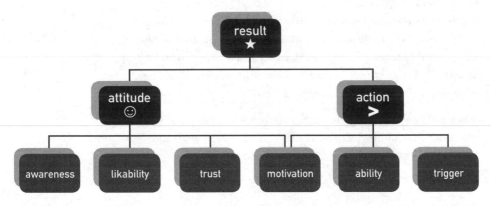

Figure 3.3: A framework for attitude and action to get a result. Action based on BJ Fogg's Behavior Model.

The rest of this book expands on these components, especially how content supports them. For now, here is a brief explanation of each:

- **Awareness:** Do users know who you are and what you stand for?
- **Likability:** Do users like, or identify with, you and what you stand for?

- **Trust:** Do users find you credible and trustworthy, especially regarding what you stand for?
- **Motivation:** Do users want to take the action you want them to take?
- **Ability:** Can users take the action easily?
- **Call:** What will inspire users to take action *now*?

This framework will help you focus on the important aspects of users, brand, forum, and timing. And, in the end, this framework comes to life through web content.

Does What We Think Really Drive What We Do?

No one knows exactly. The persuasion theory of reasoned action says that our thinking affects our actions.[1] But, the precise relationship between our thoughts and actions is not clear scientifically.

One famous clue that our thoughts affect our actions is the scientific taste test of Coke and Pepsi soft drinks. When the taste test was blind, people chose Pepsi. When the taste test was not blind, people chose Coke. Two brain scans showed that the taste test in which brands were visible actually triggered different brain activity than the blind taste test. That's potent.

To me, the theory that our thoughts affect our actions is like the theory of gravity. It makes sense and has indirect research support. However, it might be impossible to prove once and for all.

The problem? Many interactive professionals dismiss attitude as hard to measure and focus *only* on action, or behavior.

Instead, I think we should treat the rational theory like we treat gravity. We plan for it. **We don't jump out of an airplane without a parachute because gravity is "only" a theory. So, too, we need to plan for the theory that what we think affects what we do.**

USERS/CUSTOMERS

Who are you trying to reach? You can't influence people if you don't know much about them. To know who you're dealing with, learn at least *some* of the characteristics listed in **Table 3.2**. You'll gain insight into how likely it is that your users or customers will take an action or adopt an attitude. To boot, you'll learn details that will help you communicate clearly and persuasively.

Table 3.2: User/Customer Characteristics to Know

CHARACTERISTIC	DESCRIPTION
Demographics	Statistics about users such as age, income, race, education, sex, occupation
Behaviors	Users' patterns of action, such as where they shop or which websites they visit
Expectations	Users' notions of how an experience should work or flow
Role(s)	Function or responsibility (e.g., buyer, decision-maker, influencer)
Values	Users' individual, community, and cultural beliefs
Disposition	Perception(s) of your brand, topic, idea, and more

A great way to bring these characteristics to life is a *user persona*. A user persona tells the story of a fictitious user who represents the key characteristics. This story makes those characteristics easy to remember as you plan and create content. For more about using personas for web writing, check out *Letting Go of the Words* by Ginny Redish.

With this understanding of your users or customers, you can see what will help or hinder the results you want—and where to focus your influential content.

What Aligns and What Needs to Change?

When you compare what you learn about your users with the attitudes and actions you need for results, you'll find some things align well—and some don't. Grasshopper, for example, likely faced some simple alignments and gaps when it first tried to offer services to entrepreneurs. See **Table 3.3** and **Table 3.4**.

Table 3.3: Sample Alignments Between Result and Users

WE NEED USERS TO...	AND ENTREPRENEURS...	SO AN ALIGNMENT IS...
Be aware of us	Keep up with new trends and companies (Behaviors)	Reachability
Like us	Like other entrepreneurs (Disposition)	Entrepreneurship
Trust us	Support innovation (Value)	Innovation
Want to sign up	Are open to trying new things (Disposition)	Openness to change
Be *able* to sign up	Use other web-based services (Behaviors)	Web service

Table 3.4: Sample Gaps Between Result and Users

WE NEED USERS TO...	BUT ENTREPRENEURS...	SO A GAP IS...
Be aware of and like us	Don't know we exist (Disposition)	Awareness
Trust us	Are used to big brand telcos (Expectation)	Credibility
Want to sign up	Don't see an urgent need for service (Disposition)	Benefit/Need
Be *able* to sign up	Have little time and patience (Disposition)	Attention span

The alignments likely are strengths to call out in your content. The gaps are weaknesses to overcome through your content.

A famous example of overcoming a gap through content is Apple. When Apple introduced the very first iPhone, the interface was nothing like other mobile phones. Would people have the *ability* to use it? When people expected hard keys, asking them to try a tiny touchscreen was a big deal. So, did Apple bury how to use the iPhone in a user manual? No, just the opposite. Apple created videos, pictures, text, and more about using the iPhone, then used that content for advertising, buyer research, and support (**Figure 3.4**).

Figure 3.4: Example video about the iPhone touchscreen.

Now, if you see a *huge* gap, then reconsider whether you have the right result or the right users in mind. One notable exception is the health industry. Often, clinicians and public health educators face a big gap between what people *actually* think and do and what people *should* think and do for better health. In such cases, you have to spend more time up front raising awareness and educating before you can focus on action. For more, see the Timing section later in this chapter.

How to Learn about Your Users or Customers

An established organization likely has at least some research about its users, or customers. If not, you can learn what you need to know from common research techniques in user experience and marketing. Whether you do this research yourself or have someone else do it, you'll find these resources handy:

- *Mental Models* by Indi Young
- *Strategic Market Research* by Anne Beall

BRAND

Your organization's brand is its identity. It's who you are in the eyes of your users. For this book, I assume you're starting with a basic brand already—at least a name, logo, and some brand attributes. If not, consider working with a branding consultant or agency and check out these books:

- *Designing Brand Identity* by Alina Wheeler
- *BrandSimple* by Allen P. Adamson and Sir Martin Sorrell
- *Brandraising* (for nonprofits) by Sarah Durham
- *Marketing: Unmasked* (for small business) by Erik Wolf and Stephanie Frost
- *The Brand Gap* by Marty Neumeier

What about Your Brand Will Help?

Your brand can make your organization's character clear and compelling. For example, Grasshopper is trying to reach entrepreneurs, so its brand centers around entrepreneurship. The web content explains that its founders are entrepreneurs (**Figure 3.5**). That's smart because people like and trust people who are similar to them.

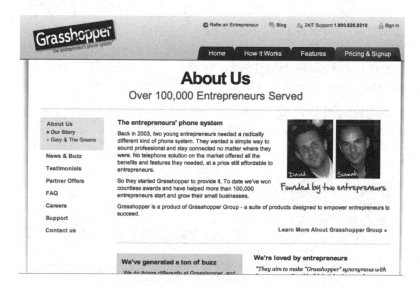

Figure 3.5: Content showcasing Grasshopper's entrepreneurial founders.

For more inspiration to bring your brand to life through content, see Chapters 4 and 5.

Ways to Learn about Your Brand

If you're new to an established brand, get to know it by talking to a brand manager or asking around for these types of documents:

- Value proposition
- Design, creative, or experience brief
- Annual report
- Mission/vision statements

TIMING

Know what's happening around you and your users to make your content relevant. Also, think about the time you'll need to influence your users' attitudes or actions.

What's Happening in the Market, Industry, or World at Large?

What are competitors doing in your market or industry? What trends are in full force? What season or time of year is it? Are any major events in the country or the world on everyone's minds? Answering these questions will help you think of ways to make your content clearly relevant. (In journalism, these ways are known as *hooks*.)

For instance, REI's home page features relevant product information that's appropriate for the time of year (**Figure 3.6**). In this example, that time of year is summer.

Figure 3.6: REI ties content into the season.

How Big Is the Gap Between What Users Think Now and What You Want Them to Think?

The bigger the gap, the longer you will need to raise awareness, become liked, earn trust, and motivate change. For example, content on the It's Your Sex Life website (sponsored by MTV and Kaiser Family Foundation) addresses teens' attitudes toward safe sex. Facts make teens aware of the truth about testing, protection, and more. The straight talk tone is likable, even hip. And, messages such as "take control" and "take charge" challenge teens to be responsible for their own decisions (**Figure 3.7**).

Figure 3.7: Content influences teens to have a responsible attitude toward sex.

How Big Is the Gap Between What Users Can Do Now and What You Want Them to Do?

The bigger the gap, the more time you will need to spend on helping people become *able* to take the action. That might mean educating people about the action, showing how other people have taken the action, and providing help or support through the action. For instance, before releasing the iPhone with a touchscreen unfamiliar to most mobile phone users, Apple spent a lot of time showing people how to use it.

How Long Do You Want Users to Commit?

When people agree to donate $20 each month for a year, they're making much more of a commitment than if they donate $20 one Saturday. The more commitment you ask of people, the greater your effort must be to influence their attitudes and actions. Stanford University psychologist BJ Fogg has identified useful tiers of commitment, which I've paraphrased here:

- **Once:** Asking for a single action or commitment, such as donating $20, no strings attached.

- **Temporarily:** Asking for an action or commitment over a time period, such as donating $20 each month for one quarter.
- **Permanently:** Asking for a lasting change or commitment, such as donating to charity from now on.

For Fogg's detailed work on time and behavior, visit the Behavior Grid at www.behaviorgrid.org.

FORUMS/CHANNELS

Websites. Blogs. Social networks. Oh my.

We're talking about the web, but that still leaves a lot of places where you can have content. You'll find a nice discussion of them in Kristina Halvorson's *Content Strategy for the Web*. Here, I highlight what to think about for influence.

Which Ones Will Connect with Your Users?

Your main presence online will likely be your website. If you have enough time and resources to consider creating content for other forums or channels, find out where your users are and, more importantly, where they respond best. For example, the niche Internet retailer FootSmart.com found that their customers are very active on Facebook but not on Twitter.

What Are the Forum Conventions?

If your organization decides to blog, learn blogging etiquette and practice first, before you go live. If you decide to have a presence on Facebook, Twitter, Flickr, YouTube, or other social networks, learn their conventions, such as what a retweet is and how often to tweet. How? The best way to learn is to observe these forums in action. Bert DuMars, Vice President of E-Business and Interactive Marketing for Newell Rubbermaid, advises *immersing* yourself in the forum conventions before putting your brand on it.[2]

What Should the Tone Be?

With blogs, user-generated content (such as reviews or comments), and social networks, you have a chance to set the tone. Tone is important to communicating your brand well. For example, the Centers for Disease Control and Prevention strives for a friendly but authoritative tone across its websites and presence on social networks. Tone also is important to encourage people to give useful comments or reviews. For some excellent examples, see the presentation "Who Rocks the Party?" by Margot Bloomstein.[3]

Don't Sponsor Content or Pay Bloggers to Post about You

Why? Because that's trying to buy, not earn, your credibility. The payoff will not be great if people know it's sponsored. The payback could be hell if people *don't* know it's sponsored. Science Blogs (owned by Seed Media), for instance, tried to introduce a food science blog sponsored by Pepsi—without disclosing it was sponsored. As a result, respected science bloggers boycotted while both Seed Media and Pepsi flailed in the flak.

For a more detailed discussion of the pros and cons, see Chris Brogan's blog post, "Differentiating Between Blogger Relations and Sponsored Content" at www.chrisbrogan.com.

INFLUENCING CONTEXT: A 10,000-FOOT VIEW OF CLOUT

We've covered much ground in this chapter. To close, let's take a bird's-eye view of achieving clout.

LEARN THE PHASES OF CLOUT

For any result, your web content must influence within the context (users, brand, timing, and forums) in three phases:

1. Raise Awareness

Your organization can't influence people who don't know what it is and what it stands for. For this phase, you need web content that shows and tells who you are in a way that attracts and appeals to people. You also can plant seeds for other people to create content—articles, reviews, and more—about you.

2. Become Liked and Trusted

People won't spend enough time with your organization to be influenced if they don't like it. People also won't consider making a change for your organization if they don't trust it. For this phase, your web content needs to demonstrate your personality, values, expertise, credibility, and more in a useful and appealing way.

3. Motivate, Inspire, and Help Action

People will not take an action—whether it's subscribe to Grasshopper or get tested for STDs—unless they want to and can do so easily. For this phase, your content has to explain how the action will meet people's needs best, offer them unique benefits, and prove that it's easy. At the right time, your web content must call people to act. Finally, your content should guide people through the action itself.

USE PRINCIPLES OF RHETORIC AND PSYCHOLOGY

To influence, your web content has much work to do. Fortunately, help is here—rhetoric and psychology. This rich mix of art and science offers plenty of ideas for compelling content. To learn more about these principles, press on to Chapter 4.

SUMMARY

The better you know context—result, users, brand, timing, and forums—the better you can plan web content that influences the context. This chapter was heavy, but it will make you stronger for the climb to clout. Now, let's move on to principles from rhetoric and psychology to help you think of content ideas.

REFERENCES

1   Hale, Jerold L., et al. "The Theory of Reasoned Action." *The Persuasion Handbook*. Dillard, James Price and Pfau, Michael, editors. 2002.

2   Bert Dumars, Social Network Marketing for Multiple Brands—How Content Is Critical to Success (presentation for Atlanta Content Strategy) at http://www.slideshare.net/bwdumars/social-media-strategy-and-tactics-across-multiple-brands-3398320

3   Margot Bloomstein, Who Rocks the Party at http://www.slideshare.net/mbloomstein/who-rocks-the-party

4 RHETORIC: THE ART OF INFLUENCE

· ·

The ancient Greeks knew more than how to wear a toga. They introduced principles of rhetoric, such as persuasive appeals, identification, repetition, and seizing the opportune moment. These principles will help your web content influence results.

...PERSUASION HAPPENS TO BE NOT A SCIENCE, BUT AN ART.

—William Bernbach, advertising mogul

Despite its practical value, rhetoric is a lost art. We don't get to learn it in school, especially in the United States. Even worse, rhetoric is sometimes mistaken for a *dark* art. Politicians abuse it by making empty promises. Let's move forward by looking back at what the ancient Greeks (and other smart rhetoricians) actually had in mind.

WHAT RHETORIC REALLY IS

The philosopher Aristotle defined rhetoric as figuring out the best way to persuade in a situation.[1] Today, Andrea Lunsford, a respected professor at Stanford University, defines rhetoric as "the art, practice, and study of human communication."[2]

Over thousands of years, smart scholars and practitioners have debated the theory and scope of rhetoric.[3] I've distilled many of the useful ideas from that debate into four principles for web content.

1. THE TRIED-AND-TRUE APPEALS

What's the number one principle of rhetoric? Aristotle would say it's not one but three—the *persuasive appeals*. He introduced them in *Rhetoric* as *ethos* (credibility), *logos* (logic), and *pathos* (emotion). This trio has shaped notions of persuasion ever since.

Aristotle insisted on always combining these appeals. In that spirit, I include them together in this first (and longest) principle of rhetoric.

A. Credibility

It's why people should trust and listen to you or your organization. Typical points of credibility include

- **Experience:** You have *a lot* of it, or your experience is specialized.
- **Success:** You've achieved something important or are having success now.
- **Reputation:** People in the community know you as having a certain characteristic, expertise, or offering.
- **Endorsement/Association:** A credible brand or person says you are credible or connects with you in a credible way.
- **Certification:** You have earned a certain security or achievement level.

- **Longevity:** You've been around for a while.
- **Similarity:** You have a lot in common with the users. (I'll discuss this more in principle 2, Irresistible Identification.)

Use Credibility at the Right Time

The less people know about you, the more you need to prove your credibility. When you're established, sometimes you need to prove that your credibility is still relevant. The trick is to convey your credibility without making people yawn.

Apply Credibility to Content

Much has changed since ancient Greek times. We communicate largely through digital content. So, let's look at how that content can show your credibility.

Quality Content Over Time

You'll build a reputation as a trusted resource if you publish consistently good content over time. It's like being the person who always says something useful. What's even better? Becoming known for a particular approach to content. Mashable, for example, built its name in the interactive design community for offering handy lists (**Figure 4.1**).

Figure 4.1: Mashable built credibility on its signature list content.

Reviews, Awards, and Other Kudos

Focus on useful praise from sources your users know and value. For instance, the household products retailer Alice.com earned features from trusted media such as *Good Housekeeping* and CNN (**Figure 4.2**).

Quotes

Pick quotes from people your users respect and can relate to. Alice rotates quotes from actual customers that describe how the service helped them save time, money, and stress (Figure 4.2).

Figure 4.2: Pertinent awards and quotes greet customers at Alice.

Partner or Advertising Affiliations

If your website has advertising, your advertisers reflect on your credibility. The design trade journal A List Apart, for example, includes only select advertisers who are respected in the design community (**Figure 4.3**).

Figure 4.3: A List Apart features quality advertisers such as Parsons: The New School for Design.

If you're not a media property, business partnerships or alliances serve a similar purpose.

Expert Contributions

If a respected expert contributes content to your website, you gain credibility. In turn, if you're invited to *be* the expert contributor, you gain credibility. American Express Open Forum, a knowledge center for small businesses, offers content from experts at Mashable and Small Business Trends (**Figure 4.4**).

Figure 4.4: American Express Open Forum includes content from outside experts.

Curated Content from Credible Sources

Curating content is showcasing good content in a unique way. When you curate content from credible sources, you enhance your own credibility. The Brain Traffic Twitter feed, for example, highlights work by content strategists around the world and commentary from industry publications (**Figure 4.5**).

Figure 4.5: Brain Traffic's Twitter feed curates content in and around content strategy.

References

When you ground your facts with references, you not only ensure you're telling the truth but also align with credible sources (**Figure 4.6**).

Figure 4.6: Centers for Disease Control and Prevention (CDC) cites sources for its facts and guidelines.

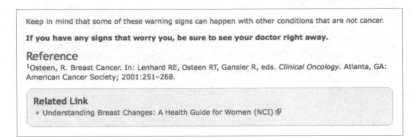

Keep in mind that some of these warning signs can happen with other conditions that are not cancer.

If you have any signs that worry you, be sure to see your doctor right away.

Reference
[1]Osteen, R. Breast Cancer. In: Lenhard RE, Osteen RT, Gansler R, eds. *Clinical Oncology*. Atlanta, GA: American Cancer Society; 2001:251–268.

Related Link
* Understanding Breast Changes: A Health Guide for Women (NCI)

Brand, Organization, or Product History

Sometimes, your organization or product has a rich and relevant history. The original Mini Cooper, for example, was designed to offer less expensive and more efficient transportation in the 1960s. Mini Cooper's website makes that story pertinent to today's environmental concerns (**Figure 4.7**).

Figure 4.7: Mini Cooper offers an appropriate brand history.

Security and Privacy Cues

When you ask people to share personal information, you need to show that your website is safe. Grasshopper.com shows security logos and a brief explanation of privacy on its registration form (**Figure 4.8**).

Figure 4.8: Grasshopper shows its safety certifications.

CREDIBILITY WORK IS BEHIND THE SCENES

Lots of the content for credibility demands background work. You or your organization have to ask, apply for, or earn much of this content.

B. Logic

It's whether your argument or reasoning is formed well (also known as being valid). At a minimum, good reasoning comprises these key elements:[4]

- **Claim:** It's what you assert to be true, such as a value proposition.

- **Evidence:** It's what supports your claim, such as facts, statistics, and testimonials.

- **Warrant:** It's why you can make the claim based on the evidence. Sometimes, the warrant is implied because it is an assumption (or set of assumptions).

Pulse Check: Website Credibility Research

When the web first became used commercially, some studies explored how people assess the credibility of a website. *Consumer Reports* sponsored perhaps the most influential study in 2002. Based on that study, *Consumer Reports* developed the following web credibility guidelines:[5]

- **Identity:** Say who you are and where you are located.

- **Advertising and Sponsorships:** Clearly distinguish between content that is advertised or sponsored and content that isn't.

- **Customer Service:** Inform people of any fees, return policies, and other information important to making shopping decisions.

- **Corrections:** Correct false, misleading, or outdated content and have a policy if someone makes a purchase using incorrect content.

These guidelines are sensible. But, almost ten years have passed. Websites are a lot different. Social networking and mobile access are on the scene. More people are using more websites more often for everything from banking to managing health records. As a result, have people's expectations changed? Has the way people evaluate website credibility evolved? I'd love to find out.

To do our part, Content Science is organizing a study and plans to report its results in 2011 at www.content-science.com.

Your argument generally is good if

- Your claim likely is true when your evidence is true.

- Users can understand the warrant quickly.

As a simple example, REI *claims* it is the first U.S.-based travel company to become 100 percent carbon neutral. The *evidence* is REI's policy of buying credits to support renewable energy (such as solar and wind). The *warrant* is that the renewable energy work neutralizes carbon emissions, so buying those credits compensates for REI's emissions.

Make Sense to Your Users

Even if you form solid logic, users make or break it. Users must accept your evidence as good evidence. For example, REI emphasizes that it buys energy credits from the respected Bonneville Environmental Foundation. Users also must share enough in common with you to understand the assumptions. In the case of REI, REI customers tend to care about the environment, and people who care about the environment likely are familiar with carbon credits.

Often, the more you ask of people's time or money, the more evidence you'll need to offer. Many people spend more time researching to buy a car than they do to buy driving gloves, for instance. That's why AutoTrader.com offers not only car advertisements but a wealth of content to research features, performance, expert opinion, and more.

Apply Logic to Content

While most web content involves at least some reasoning, certain content types lend themselves more to articulating an argument:

- Blog post
- Media article/editorial
- Expert review
- Product or service description
- White paper/fact sheet/report
- Interview

In addition, certain content types make good evidence to support an argument:

- Charts, graphs, and data visualizations
- Testimonials and case studies

For example, Mint.com offers reasoning why it is secure both in its copy and in a video interview with the CEO (**Figure 4.9**).

For a useful look at the nuances of forming arguments, I recommend *Argumentation: The Study of Effective Reasoning* by David Zarefsky and *Everything's an Argument* by Andrea Lunsford and John J. Ruszkiewicz.

Figure 4.9: Mint makes the case that it is secure.

Five Logic Mistakes You'll Regret

For airtight arguments, don't let these mistakes (also called fallacies) bubble up in your reasoning.

1. **Generalizing Hastily.** It's drawing a conclusion based on an odd example (edge case) or a very small set of examples. *SEO will double all companies' website traffic because SEO doubled her company's website traffic.*

2. **Distracting with a Red Herring.** It's making an emotionally charged point that isn't relevant. *We should spend half of our interactive budget on SEO, unless we want our competitors to trample us like they did on that customer satisfaction survey.*

3. **Confusing Cause with Correlation.** It's claiming that one event caused another *only* because the events happened at (or close to) the same time. *My company hired an SEO expert, and the next day my dog died. Hiring the SEO expert killed my dog.*

4. **Sliding Down the Slippery Slope.** It's exaggerating that a situation will lead to a catastrophic chain of events. *If you don't spend lots of money on SEO, then you'll lose all of your prospective customers, and then your sales will plummet, and then the terrorists will win.*

5. **Jumping on the Bandwagon.** It's relying *only* on the evidence that other people are doing it. *Your competitors are spending lots of money on SEO. You should, too.*

Of course, every rule is meant to be broken. Sometimes, using a fallacy is funny.

C. Emotion

It's how you tap into people's emotions to hold their interest, gain their sympathies, or motivate them to act. Appealing to emotion involves these related elements:

- **Tone:** The mood conveyed through your words, images, and other content.

- **Style:** Vivid word choice or imagery that's charged with emotion.

Let's look at a simple yet clever example from Grasshopper. Instead of a typical name, Grasshopper calls one of its voicemail plans "grow" (**Figure 4.10**). What entrepreneur doesn't aspire to grow?

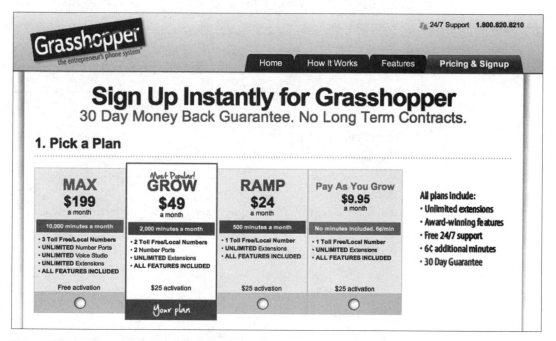

Figure 4.10: Grasshopper taps into emotion with the plan name "grow."

Handle Feeling with Care

Who determines whether emotion works? Your users. Injecting emotion into your web content is like igniting a fire. You can shine brilliantly—or burn badly. If you consider your users' cultural values and beliefs, you're more likely to shine.

In my experience with international brands, different countries and regions respond differently to emotion. Some cultures prefer subtle appeals, while others respond to bold appeals. I've shown a range in **Table 4.1**.

Table 4.1: Sample of Cultural Considerations

COUNTRY/REGION	PREFERRED STYLE	EXAMPLE
Canada and Western Europe	Subtle	We neutralize our carbon emissions.
United States	Bold	Our travel is 100% carbon neutral.
Middle East	Very bold	We're the first and best 100% carbon neutral travel company.

Apply Emotion to Content

Content offers many opportunities to charm your users' emotions.

Voice

It's the personality or feel of your content. Two very different examples are Bliss and HowStuffWorks.com. Bliss is sassy, while HowStuffWorks is dissecting (**Figure 4.11**).

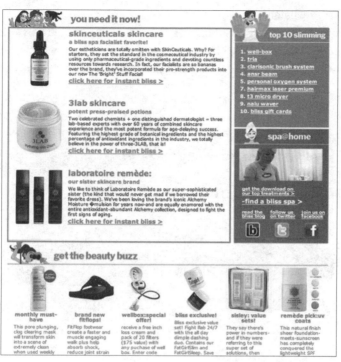

Figure 4.11: Bliss has a sassy voice, while HowStuffWorks has an analytical voice.

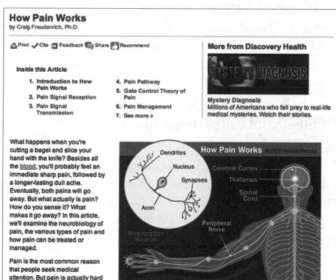

Sensory Detail

When you portray how things look, sound, smell, taste, or feel, you trigger people's gut reactions. Lindt, for instance, describes how wonderfully chocolate engages all five senses, tempting a chocoholic like me (**Figure 4.12**).

Figure 4.12: Lindt uses sensory detail to evoke emotion.

Associations with Words and Images

Beyond their literal meanings, words and images stir up feelings (also called connotations). "Grow" in the previous Grasshopper example meant not only a larger voicemail plan but also the ambition to thrive. Refer to Figure 4.10.

2. IRRESISTIBLE IDENTIFICATION

Identification is overcoming our differences to find common ground. It's the key principle to help you attract the right people. Rhetorician Kenneth Burke defined identification as "any of the wide variety of means by which an author may establish a shared sense of values, attitudes, and interests with his [or her] readers [users]."[6] When users identify with you, they're more likely to be drawn to you.

Five Rhetorical Devices You'll Love

Rhetorical devices are tools to enhance content emotionally. These are text examples, but you can apply many of these devices to images, video, or audio, too.

1. **Hyperbole.** It's over-the-top exaggeration, usually meant to be funny. *I love quality content so much that I want to marry it.*

2. **Irony.** It's when the literal and intended meaning are out of sync, often intended to be funny. *You should publish the blog post that you paid someone $10 to write for you.*

3. **Simile.** It compares unlike things. *This stagnant content is like a cesspool.*

4. **Rhetorical Question.** It's a question for dramatic effect, not asking for a literal answer. *Do we really want to keep creating terrible web content?*

5. **Personification.** It's adding personality or human qualities to a concept or object. *The website threw content from 1999 in my general direction.*

Identify on the Right Level

We connect with people who are like us on different levels.

Shallow

People relate superficially to people who share the same demographics. We can identify quickly with people who appear to be just like us. For example, the Alice home page features a thirty-something woman—a key demographic for household goods (**Figure 4.13**).

Figure 4.13: The photo of a woman represents an important demographic for Alice.

Deep

People connect more intensely to other people in a similar role or with like values, interests, and beliefs. Relating to people deeply can transcend shallow differences. In his historic campaign to become the first African American president of the United States, Barack Obama stressed change (**Figure 4.14**). That value came to life in the slogan "change we can believe in" and web content such as interviews, videos, photos, tweets, and other web content that *showed* Obama's personality and way of thinking as a change.

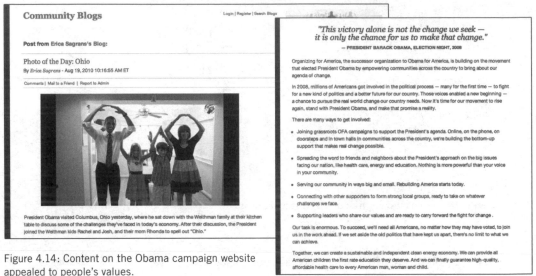

Figure 4.14: Content on the Obama campaign website appealed to people's values.

Not Everyone Will Identify with You—and That's OK

It's hard to watch people turn away from your company or cause. Even the successful Obama campaign didn't attract everyone. When you try to reach everyone, you risk reaching no one. As content marketing expert Joe Pulizzi says, "Your brand has to stand for something. If *everyone* loves you, you might be doing something wrong."[7] As long as you're attracting the people you want to attract—whether qualified leads or enthusiastic supporters—you can rest easy if someone turns away.

Apply Identification to Content

To attract people who identify with you or your organization, web content can help.

Persona/Character/Spokesperson

It's representing your organization with a person or character (or two or three) who relates well to your users. For example, HowStuffWorks offers a collection of podcasts hosted by relevant personalities. The most popular is Stuff You Should Know. On this podcast, the self-proclaimed geeks Josh and Chuck banter about, well, stuff they think other geeks should know (**Figure 4.15**).

Figure 4.15: Josh and Chuck represent geekdom for HowStuffWorks.

Another example is @sharpiesusan, a persona who embodies Sharpie on Twitter. (For more about how Sharpie's use of personas evolved, see the sidebar Sharpie's Shift from Celebrities to Personas and Users.)

User-Generated Content

Similar to personas, your users can represent you well. How? Through comments and content they contribute to your social networking space. The right potential customers will identify with your current customers. The trick is to facilitate the discussion so it stays true to your brand and your users. FootSmart, for example, carefully cultivates community on its active Facebook page (**Figure 4.16**).

Figure 4.16: FootSmart actively facilitates discussion on its Facebook page.

Cause Content

Another approach is creating content around a cause. Research from the public relations firm Edelman has found that supporting a cause could even inspire users to switch brands.[8] Select a cause that fits your brand values and your users' values. For example, REI devotes much content to environmental concerns (**Figure 4.17**).

Figure 4.17: The environment is a cause close to the hearts of many REI users and relates to REI's brand as an outdoor outfitter.

Sharpie's Shift from Celebrities to Personas and Users

David Beckham. A megacelebrity. An ideal spokesperson.

Sharpie enjoyed soccer star David Beckham's representation in several commercials. In them, Beckham signs autographs with fans' Sharpies—and becomes so enamored with the pens he humorously tries to score one for himself. While these commercials succeeded, the rise of consumer creativity and social networking inspired Sharpie to try a new approach.

Sharpie developed a *persona* on Twitter, @sharpiesusan (Susan Wassel), who shares news and tips as well as banters with Sharpie customers.

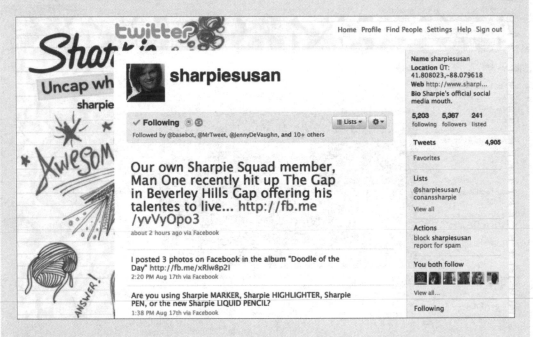

At the same time, Sharpie introduced Sharpie Uncapped (www.sharpieuncapped.com), which curates the elaborate artistic creations by Sharpie users. As Wassel notes, the effort "celebrates the amazing and inspiring things our fans are doing with our product while encouraging others to uncap their own creativity. The goal is to amplify our efforts and engage our passionate fans in the social space with compelling content."

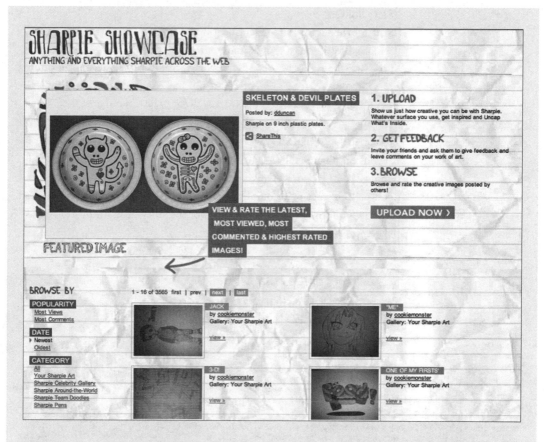

While pioneering this approach to content has meant a lot of work and a lot of lessons learned, the effort has paid off, say Wassel and Bert DuMars, Vice President of E-Business and Interactive Marketing for Newell Rubbermaid.

"The overall integrated marketing program helped us grow Sharpie into the number one writing instruments brand in North America in 2010. We have also successfully achieved a significant foothold in brand community and engagement building with our Sharpie Facebook page reaching 1.2 million fans," says DuMars.

Adds Wassel, "What we're doing is clearly resonating. We have more than a million fans on Facebook alone—highly engaged fans who comment and share in huge numbers. And, we just recently expanded the bandwidth on our blog to accommodate dramatic increases in traffic. Truth is, we're as passionate about our fans as they are about us. I think that comes through."

Story Content

Still another approach to identification is telling a story, or narrative. A story allows you to bring values to life in a memorable—even entertaining—way.[9] Because a story often involves credibility, logic, and emotion, too, it makes a strong influential impact. You can find a story in almost anything, but I find two types work well for practical purposes.

Brand/Organization Story

If you're a startup, tell the tale of solving a tough problem or making a big change to help people. Grasshopper, for example, offers the concise but compelling story of its founding (**Figure 4.18**). If you're more established, explore your history (see Credibility) or the story of an innovation or accomplishment.

About Us
Over 100,000 Entrepreneurs Served

About Us
- Our Story
- Gary & The Greens

News & Buzz

Testimonials

Partner Offers

FAQ

Careers

Support

Contact us

The entrepreneurs' phone system

Back in 2003, two young entrepreneurs needed a radically different kind of phone system. They wanted a simple way to sound professional and stay connected no matter where they were. No telephone solution on the market offered all the benefits and features they needed, at a price still affordable to entrepreneurs.

So they started Grasshopper to provide it. To date we've won countless awards and have helped more than 100,000 entrepreneurs start and grow their small businesses.

Grasshopper is a product of Grasshopper Group - a suite of products designed to empower entrepreneurs to succeed.

David   Siamak

Founded by two entrepreneurs

Learn More About Grasshopper Group »

Figure 4.18: Grasshopper tells the tale of its entrepreneurial roots.

Client/Customer Case Study

Case studies recount how you help your users. One approach is *dramatization*. For example, BooneOakley, an advertising agency in North Carolina, humorously explains why it's different (**Figure 4.19**). The agency shares the story of Billy, a typical marketing director who goes to the typical advertising agencies in New York and gets typical work—only to be fired, then untypically killed.

Figure 4.19: BooneOakley, located in North Carolina, dramatizes why it's different through the story of a marketing director.

THE STORY OF A SLIPPERY SLOPE

The BooneOakley video website employs the logical fallacy of sliding down the slippery slope to hilarious effect. See it at www.youtube.com/watch?v=Elo7Welydh8

A different approach is to present *actual customer stories*. A series of iPhone videos, for instance, showcases real users explaining how the iPhone saved the day. In one, a pilot recalls how he looked up the weather on the iPhone to help his flight avoid a three-hour delay (**Figure 4.20**).

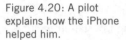
Figure 4.20: A pilot explains how the iPhone helped him.

Although Burke defined identification in the 1950s, I wonder whether he had a crystal ball that let him glimpse the 21st century. He felt identification could happen within a short paragraph, a long series of communications over time, and everything in between. So, now, let's turn to two principles of timing.

3. REPETITION THAT DOESN'T BORE OR BROADCAST

The ancient Greeks crafted creative ways of repeating ideas. Why go to such pains? Those toga-sporting orators knew that repetition helps people remember—but also risks boring them. Today, when we use tweets, emails, and ads to blast a message again, again, again, again, again, and AGAIN, our users could tune us out. So, let's take a closer look at repetition.

Three Really Is a Charm

When it comes to making the same point, three times is enough. Research everywhere from speech communication to television advertising suggests three as the magic number.[10] A challenge with web content is that we can't control *exactly* how many times a user sees or hears our message. But, we *can* control how often we publish the same message, how often we change the message, and how we bring the message to life through web content. We can avoid bombarding our users.

Apply Repetition to Content

With web content and some help from modern media, we have the power to plan our repetition wisely.

Editorial Calendar

It's a tool borrowed from journalism to plan content over time (**Figure 4.21**).[11]

	A	B	C	D	E
1		Important Dates	Blog Post	Content Type/Event #1	Content Type/Event #2
2	Week of August 16				
3	Monday, August 16, 2010				
4	Tuesday, August 17, 2010				
5	Wednesday, August 18, 2010				
6	Thursday, August 19, 2010				
7	Friday, August 20, 2010				
8					
9	Week of August 23				
10	Monday, August 23, 2010				
11	Tuesday, August 24, 2010				
12	Wednesday, August 25, 2010				
13	Thursday, August 26, 2010				
14	Friday, August 27, 2010				
15					
16	Week of August 30				
17	Monday, August 30, 2010				
18	Tuesday, August 31, 2010				
19	Wednesday, September 01, 2010				
20	Thursday, September 02, 2010				

Figure 4.21: A simple editorial calendar tracks what content to publish when.

Usually a spreadsheet or table, the exact form of an editorial calendar doesn't matter so much as the planning. When you decide in detail *what* content you will publish and *when*, you're more likely to repeat messages, topics, and themes appropriately.

For a longer look at editorial calendars for business, see "How to Put Together an Editorial Calendar for Content Marketing" by Michele Linn at Content Marketing Institute (www.contentmarketinginstitute.com).

For an examination of editorial strategy for media and entertainment, see "Exploring Editorial Strategy" by Jeffrey MacIntyre at Predicate, LLC (predicate-llc.com).

Hook

As journalism slang, it refers to why content is relevant at a particular time. A hook can help you breathe new life into your message, theme, or topic. Some examples include tying content to

- The season
- An anniversary

- A recognition, such as becoming first, most, or best
- A current event or an industry trend

For example, AOL News took the 40th anniversary of the Apollo 11 moon landing as an opportunity to reenact it through web content—videos, animation, audio, photos, and more (**Figure 4.22**).

Figure 4.22: AOL News orchestrates a virtual reenactment of the Apollo 11 moon landing on its 40th anniversary.

Amplification

It's all the ways to amplify, or enhance, your point instead of repeating it like a robot. For example, on the television show *Northern Exposure*, the poetic DJ Chris Stevens used amplification to explain the meaning of light:

"Goethe's final words: 'More light.' Ever since we crawled out of that primordial slime, that's been our unifying cry: 'More light.' Sunlight. Torchlight. Candlelight. Neon. Incandescent. Lights that banish the darkness from our caves, to illuminate our roads, the insides of our refrigerators. Big floods for the night games at Soldier Field. Little tiny flashlights for those books we read under the covers when we're supposed to be asleep. Light is more than watts and foot-candles. Light is metaphor."[12]

Classic rhetoricians used words to intensify a point. Today, we can augment an idea through web content in several ways.

Content Formats and Types

We can make points through a combination of photos, podcasts, videos, articles, and more. HowStuffWorks, for example, offers several ways to experience the danger of sharks (**Figure 4.23**).

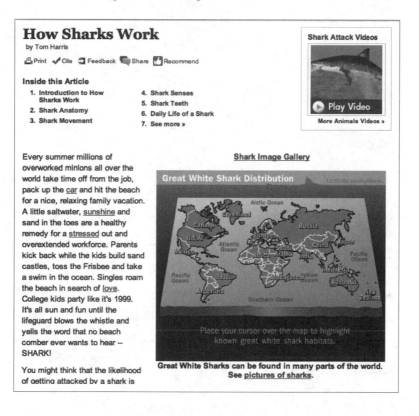

Figure 4.23: Video, photos, and text intensify the danger of sharks.

AMPLIFYING ISN'T ADDING

Amplification does not mean more web content is better. You still have to select or craft the content carefully to develop your point.

Echo

It's a phenomenon on social networking sites where other people share or restate your message or your content. When that happens, you don't have to state it yourself so often. (An extreme version of this is having something go "viral.") A case in point is CDC on Twitter and Facebook (**Figure 4.24**). When CDC posts an update, users share it with others.

Figure 4.24: Users share CDC's updates on social networks.

Three Devices to Repeat Words Remarkably

. . . .

The ancient Greeks had all kinds of devices for repeating words. Consider these three for emphasis.

1. **Anaphora.** Repeating a word or phrase at the beginning of each clause. *Content attracts people. Content motivates people. Content guides people.*

2. **Antistasis.** Repetition of a word in a different or contrary sense. *Don't be content with your lackluster content.*

3. **Diacope.** Repetition of a word or phrase broken up by one or more intervening words. *Content, content, content—where will we get the content?*

4. THE OPPORTUNE MOMENT!

Time. A concept so complex, the Greeks had not one, but two, words for it. *Chronos* meant chronological time, such as morning, noon, and night. *Kairos* meant the opportune moment. It's the *right time* to say something in the *right way.* I think of it as the ideal time to ask people to change their viewpoint or to take an action. The key is to ask when people are ready.

Don't Ask Too Much Too Soon or Too Often

Ancient rhetoricians felt the opportune moment was *special*. It didn't come along everyday. That's worth remembering when we're tempted to press users quickly for personal information or bombard them with emails and tweets. As a simple example from Content Science, we send an email once per *quarter* to our email list. Our email open rate is 50 percent. When I shared that high rate with a marketing friend, she nearly fell out of her chair.

Ask Clearly

People won't respond how you'd like if they aren't sure what you want. For instance, Content Science assessed this original version of a CDC website about travel health. We found some quality content to help travelers stay healthy. But, what CDC recommended people should *do* was vague (**Figure 4.25**). CDC even tested this website with real users, most of whom were very interested in the content but confused about what to do next. (For a case study of how we improved this website, see Chapter 5.)

React to a Crisis Promptly

A hurricane strikes. A CEO resigns. A damaging video goes viral. Sometimes, the opportune moment arises because of a shocking event. When I worked for CDC, I occasionally took a turn responding to everything from bioterrorism to SARS. I can assure you it's much better to say *something* trustworthy sooner, not later, so people don't panic or spread rumors.

Health Information for Travelers to Brazil

On This Page

- Travel Notices in Effect
- Safety and Security Abroad
- Preparing for Your Trip to Brazil
- Other Diseases Found in Tropical South America
- Staying Healthy During Your Trip
- Aft...

Travel Notices in Effect

- Update: Dengue, Tropical and Subtropical Regions June 02, 2010
- 2010 Measles Update April 22, 2010
- 2009 H1N1 Flu: Global Situation March 29, 2010
- Yellow Fever in Brazil March 02, 2010

Top of Page

Safety and Security Abroad

- Registration of Traveler Emergency Contact and Itinerary Information Jun
- Transportation Security Administration
- U.S. Department of State

Top of Page

Preparing for Your Trip to Brazil

Before visiting Brazil, you may need to get the following vaccinations vaccine-preventable diseases and other diseases you might be at risk destination: (Note: Your doctor or health-care provider will determine what on factors such as your health and immunization history, areas of the country planned activities.)

To have the most benefit, see a health-care provider at least 4–6 weeks befo time for your vaccines to take effect and to start taking medicine to prevent

Even if you have less than 4 weeks before you leave, you should still see a h needed vaccines, anti-malaria drugs and other medications and information a yourself from illness and injury while traveling.

CDC recommends that you see a health-care provider who specializes in Trave travel medicine clinic near you. If you have a medical condition, you should a plans with any doctors you are currently seeing for other medical reasons.

If your travel plans will take you to more than one country during a single trip health-care provider know so that you can receive the appropriate vaccination of your destinations. Long-term travelers, such as those who plan to work or need additional vaccinations as required by their employer or school.

Be sure your routine vaccinations are up-to-date. Check the links belo vaccinations adults and children should get.

Routine vaccines, as they are often called, such as for influenza, chickenpo measles/mumps/rubella (MMR), and diphtheria/pertussis/tetanus (DPT) are gi life; see the childhood and adolescent immunization schedule and routine adul schedule.

Routine vaccines are recommended even if you do not travel. Although childho measles, rarely occur in the United States, are still common in many par traveler who is not vaccinated would be at risk for infection.

Vaccine-Preventable Diseases

Vaccine recommendations are based on the best available risk information. Please note that the level of risk for vaccine-preventable diseases can change at any time.

Vaccination or Disease	Recommendations or Requirements for Vaccine-Preventable Diseases
Routine	Recommended if you are not up-to-date with routine shots such as, measles/mumps/rubella (MMR) vaccine, diphtheria/pertussis/tetanus (DPT) vaccine, poliovirus vaccine, etc.
Yellow Fever	Brazil does not require travelers entering Brazil to present proof of yellow fever vaccination. CDC yellow fever vaccination recommendation for travelers to Brazil: For all travelers ≥9 months of age going to the following areas at risk for yellow fever transmission, including the ENTIRE states of Acre, Amapá, Amazonas, Distrito Federal (including the capital city of Brasília), Goiás, Maranhão, Mato Grosso, Mato Grosso do Sul, Minas Gerais, Pará, Rondônia, Roraima, and Tocantins; only designated areas of the following states: Bahia, Paraná, Piauí, Rio Grande do Sul, Santa Catarina, and São Paulo (refer to the Updated CDC Yellow Fever Map for Brazil to see areas of these states with risk for yellow fever transmission). Vaccination is recommended for travelers visiting Iguassu Falls. Vaccination is NOT recommended for travel to the following coastal cities: Rio de Janeiro, São Paulo, Salvador, Recife, and Fortaleza. *(Updated March 10, 2010)* Vaccination should be given 10 days before travel and at 10 year intervals if there is on-going risk. Find an authorized U.S. yellow fever vaccination clinic.
Hepatitis A or immune globulin (IG)	Recommended for all unvaccinated people traveling to or working in countries with an intermediate or high level of hepatitis A virus infection (see map) where exposure might occur through food or water. Cases of travel-related hepatitis A can also occur in travelers to developing countries with "standard" tourist itineraries, accommodations, and food consumption behaviors.
Hepatitis B	Recommended for all unvaccinated persons traveling to or working in countries with intermediate to high levels of endemic HBV transmission (see map), especially those who might be exposed to blood or body fluids, have sexual contact with the local population, or be exposed through medical treatment (e.g., for an accident).
Typhoid	Recommended for all unvaccinated people traveling to or working in Tropical South America, especially if staying with friends or relatives or visiting smaller cities, villages, or rural areas where exposure might occur through food or water.
Rabies	Recommended for travelers spending a lot of time outdoors, especially in rural areas, involved in activities such as bicycling, camping, or hiking. Also recommended for travelers with significant occupational risks (such as veterinarians), for long-term travelers and expatriates living in areas with a significant risk of exposure, and for travelers involved in any activities that might bring them into direct contact with bats, carnivores, and other mammals. Children are considered at higher risk because they tend to play with animals, may receive more severe bites, or may not report bites.

Malaria

Areas of Brazil with Malaria: States of Acre, Rondônia, Amapá, Amazonas, Roraima, and Tocantins. Parts of states of Maranhão (western part), Mato Grosso (northern part), and Pará (except Belem City). Also present in urban areas, including large cities such as Porto Velho, Boa Vista, Macapa, Manaus, Santarem, and Maraba, where the transmission occurs on the periphery of these cities. Malaria in Iguassu Falls.

If you will be visiting an area of Brazil with malaria, you will need to discuss with your doctor the best ways for you to avoid getting sick with malaria. Ways to prevent malaria include the following:

- Taking a prescription antimalarial drug
- Using insect repellent and wearing long pants and sleeves to prevent mosquito bites
- Sleeping in air-conditioned or well-screened rooms or using bednets

All of the following antimalarial drugs are equal options for preventing malaria in Brazil: Atovaquone/proguanil, doxycycline, or mefloquine. For detailed information about each of these drugs, see Table 2-23: Drugs used in the prophylaxis of malaria. For information that can help you and your doctor decide which of these drugs would be best for you, please see Choosing a Drug to Prevent Malaria.

Note: Chloroquine is NOT an effective antimalarial drug in Brazil and should not be taken to prevent malaria in this region.

To find out more information on malaria throughout the world, you can use the interactive CDC malaria map. You can search or browse countries, cities, and place names for more specific malaria risk information and the recommended prevention medicines for that area.

Malaria Contact for Health-Care Providers
For assistance with the diagnosis or management of suspected cases of malaria, call the CDC Malaria Hotline: **770-488-7788** (M-F, 9 am–5 pm, Eastern time). For emergency consultation after hours, call **770-488-7100** and ask to speak with a CDC Malaria Branch clinician.

Figure 4.25: A website vaguely asks people to travel healthy.

Apply the Opportune Moment to Content

On the web, our content can seize *kairos* in several ways.

Advertisement

Chapter 1 noted how ads annoy people. What if ads were more relevant to a website's topics and users? For example, *National Geographic*'s readers typically care about the environment. An IBM ad stays pertinent with the message to "build a smarter planet" (**Figure 4.26**).

Figure 4.26: A relevant ad on the *National Geographic* website.

Call to Action

Clear, concise, and earnest—what makes a good call to action. Mayo Clinic Health Manager offers an unmistakable invitation to begin the sign-up process with a button labeled "Get started now" (**Figure 4.27**).

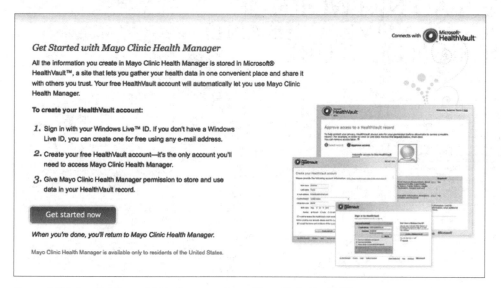

Figure 4.27: An effective call to action appears on Mayo Clinic Health Manager.

The Deck: An Innovative System of Advertising

The Deck is a unique advertising system that ensures quality, relevant ads for publications in the creative industry such as Jeffrey Zeldman's *A List Apart*. Jim Coudal, co-creator of The Deck and president of Coudal Partners, explains the system this way:

"The Deck takes the approach that to be successful we need to address the needs of all three parties involved in the advertising:

- **Site publishers** get vetted, truly relevant ads in a manageable size and without animation or other tricks.

- **Advertisers** get an uncluttered impression to an involved and curious audience.

- **Readers** get ads that don't insult them about relevant products while the sites they like to read can write and post more with the financial support of the network.

Too much of current online advertising does not treat all three parties as equally important. It's that balance that makes The Deck work so well for publishers, advertisers, and readers."

Instruction

Sometimes, helping people act requires more than a well-labeled button. In that case, contextual instructions come to the rescue. The Mayo Clinic Health Manager shown in Figure 4.27 includes simple instructions. As another example, Grasshopper offers plainly worded instructions to make a referral (**Figure 4.28**).

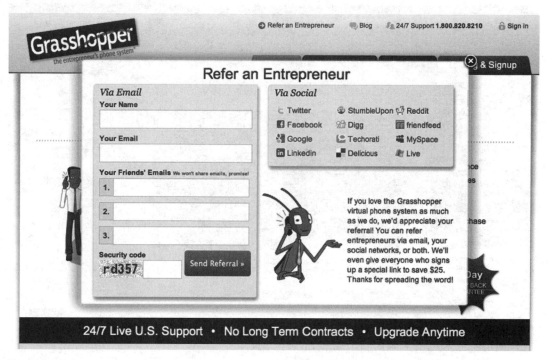

Figure 4.28: Grasshopper explains how to refer someone.

Crisis Response

How can you respond aptly? By planning for crisis situations. You can't prepare for the exact crisis, but you can think of possible crises and have a plan that answers questions like these:

- Where will we publish a response?
- Who should write and approve a response?
- If we need extra people to help us monitor and respond to questions on social networking, how will we get those people?

- What are examples of a good response?
- What style of response is appropriate for our users and our brand?

For example, when his popular wine website Cork'd was hacked, Gary Vaynerchuk didn't hide his head in the sand or scramble. Instead, he reacted with a truthful, even funny, video (**Figure 4.29**).

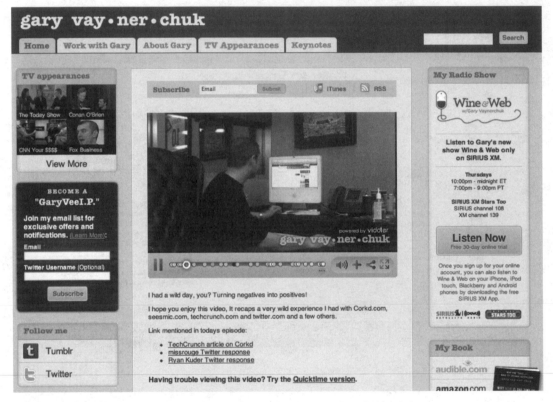

Figure 4.29: Gary Vaynerchuk reacts in a lighthearted way to the hacking of his website.

The CDC responds in a different style to a different crisis—a *salmonella* outbreak in eggs. A no-nonsense daily summary explains the latest status and what people should do about it (**Figure 4.30**).

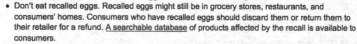

Investigation Update: Multistate Outbreak of Human *Salmonella* Enteritidis Infections Associated with Shell Eggs

August 27, 2010

On This Page

Investigation of the Outbreak | Laboratory Testing | Recall Information |
Clinical Features/Signs and Symptoms | Advice to Consumers | General Information |
Additional Resources | CDC's Role in Food Safety | Previous Updates

Today's Highlights

- From May 1 to August 25, 2010, approximately 1,470 reported illnesses were likely to be associated with this outbreak.
- FDA testing identified *Salmonella* in egg farm environmental samples.
- Don't eat recalled eggs. Recalled eggs might still be in grocery stores, restaurants, and consumers' homes. Consumers who have recalled eggs should discard them or return them to their retailer for a refund. A searchable database of products affected by the recall is available to consumers.
- Individuals who think they might have become ill from eating recalled eggs should consult their health care providers.

Figure 4.30: CDC cuts to the chase of a disease crisis.

WHEN TO USE WHAT PRINCIPLES

Aristotle advocated applying a *mix* of influential techniques. Getting the mix right is an art. Without it, users will feel bored, manipulated, or pressured. Indeed, getting the mix wrong will make your results *worse* than if you use no techniques.[13]

The right mix of principles depends largely on the context. So, let's map these principles to context—the phases of clout (**Figure 4.31**).

	Phase 1 Raise Awareness	Phase 2 Become Liked & Trusted	Phase 3 Motivate, Inspire, & Help Action
1A. Credibility	✓	✓	
1B. Logic	✓	✓	✓
1C. Emotion	✓	✓	✓
2. Identification		✓	✓
3. Repetition	✓		✓
4. The Opportune Moment			✓

Figure 4.31: A guide to using rhetorical principles to achieve clout.

In the first two phases, influencing people's *attitude* is critical, so rely on principles that establish your credibility, likability, and trustworthiness. As you enter the third phase, use principles that influence people's *actions*.

A basic example is that Grasshopper emphasizes its credibility through showing awards, quotes, and a guarantee on its Features page. However, on the Sign Up page, Grasshopper does not include content about credibility. Instead, the page focuses on guiding people to subscribe (**Figure 4.32**).

Figure 4.32: Grasshopper uses different rhetorical principles at different times to support attitude and action.

For ideas to plan the right mix of principles for specific situations, see Chapter 6.

SUMMARY

Rhetoric is not a dark art and should no longer be a lost art. Ancient rhetoric offers creative guidance to turn your modern web content into a source of clout—and consequently get results. The art is in combining rhetorical principles well. But, that's not all you need. Turn the page for four more principles grounded in science.

REFERENCES

1 Aristotle, *Rhetoric*

2 Andrea Lunsford, http://www.stanford.edu/dept/english/courses/sites/lunsford/pages/defs.htm

3 Patricia Bizzell, *The Rhetorical Tradition* (Bedford/St. Martin's, 2000)

4 David Zarefsky, *Argumentation: The Study of Effective Reasoning* (The Teaching Company Limited Partnership, 2005)

5 Consumer Reports, WebWatch, Credibility Campaign at http://www.consumerwebwatch.org/consumer-reports-webwatch-guidelines.cfm

6 Kenneth Burke, *A Rhetoric of Motives* (University of California Press, 1969)

7 Joe Pulizzi, Higher Purpose Content Marketing at http://www.slideshare.net/juntajoe/higher-purpose-content-marketing-atlanta-content-strategy-meetup

8 Despite Prolonged Global Recession, an Increasing Number of People Are Spending on Brands That Have Social Purpose at http://www.edelman.com/news/ShowOne.asp?ID=222

9 Colleen Jones, Become an Interactive Storyteller at http://www.imediaconnection.com/content/18041.imc

10 Herbert Krugman, "Why Three Exposures May Be Enough," Journal of Advertising Research, 12, 6 (1972): 11-14

11 Michele Linn, How to Put Together an Editorial Calendar for Content Marketing at http://www.contentmarketinginstitute.com/wp-content/uploads/2010/08/EditorialCalendar.jpg

12 Amplification at http://grammar.about.com/od/ab/g/amplification.htm

13 BJ Fogg, *Persuasive Technology: Using Computers to Change What We Think and Do* (Morgan Kaufmann, 2002)

5 PSYCHOLOGY: THE SCIENCE OF INFLUENCE

• •

We have modern science to thank for more insight into influence. Over time, science has discovered principles such as framing, metaphor, reciprocity, and social proof. These principles can help your web content influence results.

SCIENCE MAY SET LIMITS TO KNOWLEDGE, BUT SHOULD NOT SET LIMITS TO IMAGINATION.

—Bertrand Russell, philosopher and Nobel Peace Prize winner

Scientific research tells us a lot about how we're influenced. But, we don't learn about it in Psychology 101. And, people sometimes mistakenly believe science is a wet blanket on creativity. Let's right these wrongs by touring some of psychology's key principles of influence. Along the way, we'll apply them to web content—without dampening our creative sizzle.

WHAT PSYCHOLOGY *REALLY* IS

Science, at its heart, is very practical. Philosopher George Santayana described science as "nothing but developed perception, interpreted intent, [and] common sense rounded out and minutely articulated." Science helps us understand the whys and wherefores of what we observe. The *science* of mind and behavior is psychology.[1]

Compared to rhetoric, psychology is very young. The field's piles of research, however, offer a wealth of insight into what influences our minds. For our tour, I've selected four principles important to web content.

If I had to name a theme for these principles, I'd say *shortcut*. People don't have the time to think deeply about every little decision. Often without realizing it, people rely on these principles as timesavers. That's why it's so important to use these principles appropriately. (For more about ethics, see Chapter 11.)

1. FRAMING: GUIDING ATTENTION

A frame is a set of expectations, values, and assumptions that acts like a filtering lens. It leads us to see certain details and not others. As a simple example, let's say we're working with a project manager and a creative director. We have certain expectations for each role. If the project manager didn't create a project timeline, we'd notice and probably complain. If a creative director didn't create a project timeline, however, we probably wouldn't notice.

Framing is packaging an idea, issue, or choice in terms of the frame. Framing can lead people to understand a concept quickly and even favorably. For example, if we described an idea to a project manager, we might stress that it saves time, avoids rework, and increases efficiency. In fact, that's exactly how 37signals talks about its project management software, Basecamp (**Figure 5.1**).

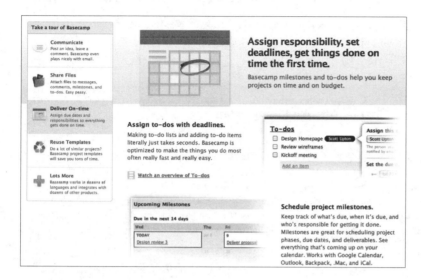

Figure 5.1: Basecamp taps into a project manager's frame of reference.

USE "LOSS" LANGUAGE CAREFULLY

People will respond to the same choice differently when it is framed in different terms. Research suggests that a negative frame, especially describing a "loss," prompts a powerful emotional reaction in people.[2] It's so strong that people will even make a risky choice to avoid feeling the loss. The excellent book *How We Decide* describes it this way:

"This human foible is known as the framing effect…the effect helps explain why people are much more likely to buy meat when it's labeled *85 percent lean* instead of *15 percent fat*. And why twice as many patients opt for surgery when told there's an 80 percent chance of their surviving instead of a 20 percent chance of their dying."[3]

Now, negative frames aren't always bad. They simply spark a lot of emotional brain activity, so they're like playing with fire. Consider these statements:

1. If you improve your search engine optimization (SEO), you will gain 5,000 new customers each year.

2. If you do not improve your search engine optimization (SEO), your company will lose 5,000 new customers each year.

From a framing perspective, statement 2 is more explosive.

So, be extra careful with negative frames. Save them for points that deserve urgent attention and a strong response. (See my discussion of ethics in Chapter 11.)

From Mass Media to New Media: Altering the Agenda

In media, politics, and public relations, one aspect of framing is *agenda setting*, or influencing what stories the media covers and, consequently, what people think about.[4] The *New York Times*, CNN, and other mass media outlets cover certain stories but not others, for example. And, within a story, mass media includes certain details and not others. So, the theory goes, people are more likely to think or chat about the stories and details that mass media covers. Whether you view agenda setting as a conspiracy or as gatekeeping, it happens because it's not possible to talk about *all* things at *all* times with *all* the detail.

Or is it?

Websites, blogs, and social networking—together known as new media—are changing the agenda. To what extent? We don't know yet. Research shows that new media and mass media, at the very least, inform each other. Research also suggests that when mass media doesn't cover stories or covers them late, new media still gives them attention. To boot, new media often provides more details about a story than mass media.[5]

Clearly, this area is one to watch. We need more research to understand how new media influences what people think about current events and political issues.

PREPARE WITH PRIMING

Related to framing, *priming* is another subtle way to get people's attention. It's introducing words, images, or ideas now to influence people's choices a little later. For example, asking people the day before an election whether they intend to vote can increase the chance they'll vote by up to 25 percent.[6] The reason priming works is we tend to act on what we remember easily.

To kick priming up a notch, you can address how to act on the choice. In the voting example, if you also showed people a map pointing out where they should go to vote, you'd further boost the chance they'll vote. As *Nudge* says, "Often we can do more to facilitate good behavior by removing some small obstacle than by trying to shove people in a certain direction."[7]

APPLY FRAMING TO CONTENT

Web content offers many opportunities to put framing to work.

Theme / Key Messages

When CDC decided to redesign its Travelers' Health website (mentioned in Chapter 4), I advised on an approach to the content. CDC wanted to convey the risk travelers face so they take the right precautions—but not to the point that people fear traveling. One recommendation I made was framing the travel precautions as smart planning to ensure business remains productive and vacation stays fun. You can see a rough concept of this approach in **Figure 5.2**.

Figure 5.2: Positive key messages convey that travel precautions are important but not scary.

Curation

For years, Starbucks has curated music that reflects its brand and cultural perspective. Starbucks created its unique frame of the musical world, and the frame resonated with customers. Starbucks even released its own successful CDs and sponsored a satellite radio channel. Now that Starbucks offers free wireless Internet access to customers, the coffee brand has released its own digital network. On it, Starbucks curates exclusive content from the *New York Times*, Apple, and other select publishers.[8] This network is Starbuck's frame of the digital world.

OPEN Forum by American Express uses curation to frame the digital world for small business. Specifically, the Idea Hub features content from select business owners and industry experts about pertinent topics (**Figure 5.3**).

Figure 5.3: American Express curates quality content for small businesses.

Claim and Evidence

The website for Pickens Plan, an energy proposal advocated by philanthropist T. Boone Pickens, frames America's dependency on oil negatively with the *claim* "America is addicted to foreign oil." In explaining the need for a plan, the content frames the *evidence* with loss language:

"In addition to putting our security in the hands of potentially unfriendly and unstable foreign nations, we spent $475 billion on foreign oil in 2008 alone. That's money taken out of our economy and sent to foreign nations, and it will continue to drain the life from our economy for as long as we fail to stop the bleeding."[9]

This negative language is strong but appropriate for a serious issue. (For more about claim and evidence in logic, see Chapter 4.)

Poll

We easily find poll widgets on websites and on social networks such as LinkedIn. On LinkedIn, you can quickly create your own polls (**Figure 5.4**).

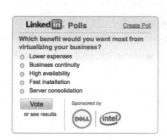

Figure 5.4: Polls appear regularly on websites such as CNN.com and LinkedIn.

I'm not aware of anyone intentionally using polls to influence. After reviewing research about priming, I believe that a poll could serve as an excellent reminder. For example, when flu season nears, a poll that asks "Do you plan to get a flu shot?" could encourage people to get one.

Reminder and Instruction

Is your Body Mass Index healthy? Is it time for your kids' shots? When did you last visit the dentist? What does your insurance cover? Your family's health information adds up to a lot of content to manage. Electronic health records can help get it under control. Imagine Mint.com for your health.

One benefit of electronic health records (EHRs) is reminding us of healthy behaviors, such as keeping our checkup appointments. The Mayo Clinic Health Manager, for example, highlights upcoming medical visits on its dashboard. What would make this reminder even better would be an option to receive it via email or text (**Figure 5.5**).

Figure 5.5: An EHR reminds me of an upcoming medical appointment.

To boot, health records can help us actually do healthy behaviors. For example, Mayo Clinic Health Manager offers a wizard that guides you through preparing for an appointment. One feature is compiling relevant sections of your personal health content so that you can bring it or send it to the doctor (**Figure 5.6**).

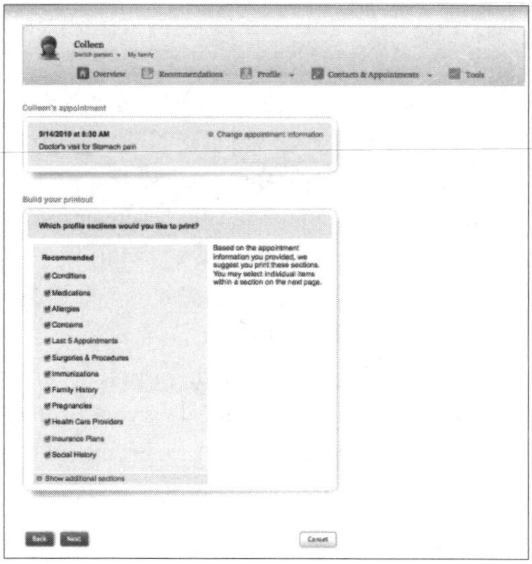

Figure 5.6: An EHR helps me get ready for the medical appointment.

Reminder and instruction matter beyond electronic health records, too. In the Travelers' Health project I mentioned under Theme, we paid close attention to instruction. Research had shown travelers were confused about *where* to get travel immunizations. The best place to get them is a travel health clinic, not a personal physician. My content recommendations stressed going to the travel health clinic and suggested ways to make finding travel clinics easier. This approach tested well with users[10] (**Figure 5.7**).

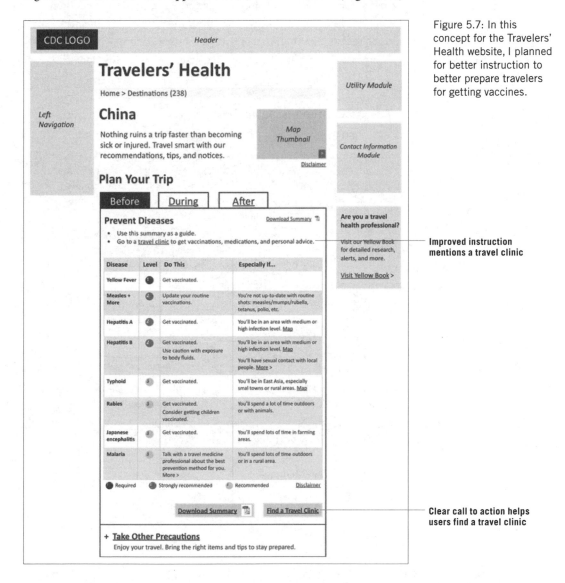

Figure 5.7: In this concept for the Travelers' Health website, I planned for better instruction to better prepare travelers for getting vaccines.

2. METAPHOR: A TIE THAT BINDS

Metaphor. Isn't that pretty language that makes a comparison, such as "Shall I compare thee to a summer's day?"[11] Yes, and it's *more*, psychologists and linguists have learned. Cognitive scientist Steven Pinker says "metaphor really is a key to explaining thought and language."[12] More specifically, consumer psychology experts Gerald Zaltman and Lindsay Zaltman say metaphors are "basic categories of patterned thinking and decision making."[13] Metaphors are the way we think and talk about our world. This research team even thinks that metaphors resonate more deeply than archetypes, a staple of marketing strategy (see the following sidebar).

7 Research-Proven Metaphors

The innovative research team of Gerald Zaltman and Lindsay Zaltman have found these metaphors to be the most common and compelling around the world. They've made the basic list freely available. (The examples noted below are simply my opinion.) For their take on discovering and using metaphors, get *Marketing Metaphoria*.

1. **Balance**. Includes the ideas of equilibrium, adjusting, maintaining or offsetting forces, and things as they should be.
   Example: Make It Right (makeitrightnola.org)

2. **Transformation**. Involves changing states or status.
   Example: Mint.com

3. **Journey**. Addresses how the past, present, and future meet.
   Example: Your Life, Your Money (www.pbs.org/your-life-your-money/)

4. **Container**. Involves keeping things in and keeping things out.
   Example: Shoeboxed.com

5. **Connection**. Encompasses feelings of belonging or exclusion.
   Example: American Express OPEN Forum (Connectodex)

6. **Resource**. Involves acquisitions and their consequences.
   Example: TED.com (ideas worth spreading)

7. **Control**. Covers mastery, vulnerability, and well-being.
   Example: Livestrong.com

Tactically, metaphor often connects new or abstract ideas to something people already know. This connection helps people understand the ideas faster. That's especially helpful for technology, which changes quickly. Interaction design expert Dan Saffer has even said "everything one says about the computer is metaphor."[14] For example, when Internet use spread in the late 1990s, the term "web page" described a website screen in terms of something familiar—a paper page. It's not really a page, though, so academics wanted to call the website screen a "node." Which term caught on?

USE METAPHORS SPARINGLY

Psychologists and English professors agree that less is more. If you use too many metaphors, you risk confusing people. Focus more on selecting the *right* metaphor and reinforcing it different ways. For example, the name Make It Right for a foundation suggests restoring or returning to balance. The website's references to *rebuilding* and *renewed* subtly support the metaphor (**Figure 5.8**).

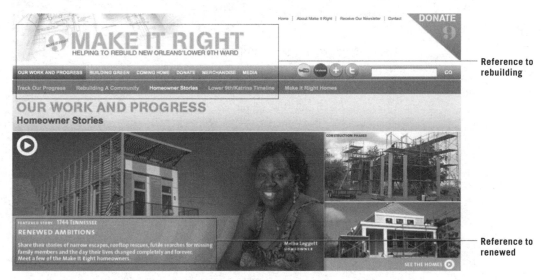

Figure 5.8: The Make It Right Foundation uses metaphor subtly but effectively.

BUILD ON METAPHORS PEOPLE ALREADY USE

Because metaphors are so vital to how we think and talk, your users say them to describe their needs and your industry. As you research and communicate with your current users—or the users you want to attract—take note of the words and phrases they use. When it comes to the complexities of finance, for example, people might feel "stuck" or eager to "turn over a new leaf" or ready for a "fresh start." The personal finance service Mint.com taps into that metaphorical language brilliantly by its name alone, which suggests

- Herbal leaf known for its *fresh* smell and taste.
- Source of *new* money.

The name also happens to be short for the original name, Money Intelligence. (We should all be so lucky with our abbreviations.)

APPLY METAPHOR TO CONTENT

We can use the mighty metaphor almost anywhere in our web content to make us memorable and likable. Here are a few examples.

Name, Message, Call to Action

As the name implies, Designzillas compares its web design agency to the Japanese monster (and sometimes hero) Godzilla. The agency sticks to this single metaphor throughout the concise site with copy and graphics (**Figure 5.9**).

This metaphor will make you laugh with messages and calls to action such as

- Is your website stuck in the stone age?
- We keep our clients on top of the food chain.
- Our agency has evolved into fire-breathing web designers.
- We are black belts in web-kwon-do.
- Call us today! We don't bite.

While funny and creative, this metaphor also positions Designzillas as a supernatural hero ready to rescue a client in need. That positioning taps into a deeper metaphor of transformation (refer to the sidebar entitled "7 Research-Proven Metaphors").

Figure 5.9: Designzillas draws on one metaphor consistently.

Organization Story

Heroic metaphor is also prominent in the story of Adam and Eric, the founders of method home care products. The story compares the founders to accidental superheroes (**Figure 5.10**).

our story

the proud brainparents of method and the very first people against dirty®.

Meet Adam Lowry and Eric Ryan, proud brainparents of method and the very first people against dirty®. Despite founding one of the fastest-growing private companies in America, and single-handedly turning the consumer-packaged-goods industry on its head, these two former roommates are quick to tell you that they're no heroes. And that's true. They're SUPER-heroes.* And like every great superhero, they gained their powers after being exposed to toxic ingredients. Cleaning supplies, to be precise. But rather than turning them green or granting them the ability to talk to fish, Eric and Adam's toxic exposure gave them something even better. An idea.

Eric knew people wanted cleaning products they didn't have to hide under their sinks. And Adam knew how to make them without any dirty ingredients. Their powers combined, they set out to save the world and create an entire line of home care products that were more powerful than a bottle of sodium hypochlorite. Gentler than a thousand puppy licks. Able to detox tall homes in a single afternoon.

Figure 5.10: Metaphor equates Adam and Eric to superheroes.

The founders "are quick to tell you that they're no heroes. And that's true. They're SUPER-heroes. And like every great superhero, they gained their powers after being exposed to toxic ingredients. Cleaning supplies, to be precise. But rather than turning them green or granting them the ability to talk to fish, Eric and Adam's toxic exposure gave them something even better. An idea.

"Eric knew people wanted cleaning products they didn't have to hide under their sinks. And Adam knew how to make them without any dirty ingredients. Their powers combined, they set out to save the world and create an entire line of home care products that were more powerful than a bottle of sodium hypochlorite. Gentler than a thousand puppy licks. Able to detox tall homes in a single afternoon."[15]

3. SOCIAL PROOF: THE VALUE OF REFERRALS

When people follow the crowd rather than decide completely on their own, social proof is in action.[16] If I see that many people are getting flu shots, for example, then I'm more likely to get a flu shot. We tend to believe other people have thought about the decision, so we don't have to.

In *Nudge*, Richard H. Thaler and Cass R. Sunstein give dozens of social proof examples across business, politics, health, and more. One of their striking examples is an elaborate study by Matthew Salganik of music downloads. The study found that

"individuals were far more likely to download songs that had been previously downloaded in significant numbers, and far less likely to download songs that had not been as popular. Most strikingly, the success of songs was quite unpredictable...the identical song could be a hit or a failure simply because other people, at the start, were seen to choose to have downloaded it or not."[17]

USERS MUST IDENTIFY WITH THE CROWD

People will be less likely to go with the crowd if they don't identify with the other people *in* the crowd.[18] If I see that the people getting flu shots are mostly gray-haired men, for example, then I won't be as quick to get one. I'll wonder whether the shot is really for someone like me. For web content, the more detail you share about who the crowd is, the more identification will affect your users. (For more about identification, see Chapter 4.)

APPLY SOCIAL PROOF TO CONTENT

Content demonstrates social proof in many ways to show we're credible and also motivates action.

Case Studies, Quotes, and Testimonials

We discussed this content in Chapter 4 as a way to build credibility. This content also shows social support. Choose your case studies, quotes, or testimonials carefully so they represent the users that you want to attract. If users don't identify with the people you feature, this content has less impact. OPEN Forum, for example, features small businesses ranging from restaurants to alpaca farmers. This variety helps ensure the case studies will resonate with users (**Figure 5.11**).

Figure 5.11: A range of case studies on OPEN Forum will resonate with a range of small business owners.

Reviews

User-generated content, such as reviews, also demonstrate social proof. Reviews suggest the popularity of a popsicle maker on Williams-Sonoma. com, for example (**Figure 5.12**).

Figure 5.12: A popular product has earned hundreds of favorable reviews.

But, what if reviewing behavior is arbitrary, like the music download research suggests, and leaves a lot of products with no reviews? To balance reviewing behavior, e-retailers such as Eddie Bauer are nudging people to give reviews through reminders and discount incentives (**Figure 5.13**).

Figure 5.13: Reminders and discounts nudge people to give reviews.

Now, what if a review doesn't reflect the viewpoint or situation of most users? If users don't identify with the reviewer, the review has less impact. To help keep reviews relevant, Amazon introduced a feature that allows people to judge the quality of reviews (**Figure 5.14**).

> If they do make a new version of the Urban Pal,
>
> **Help other customers find the most helpful reviews**
> Was this review helpful to you?
> Yes   No
>
> 6 of 6 people found the following review helpful:
> ★★★★★ **a nice alternative to pepper spray,**

Figure 5.14: Review ratings allow users to keep reviews relevant.

Followers, Likes, Votes, Signups

A staple of social networks (such as Twitter, Facebook, and LinkedIn), this content shows connection to or support from other people. Pickens Plan, for example, showcases its following on Twitter and Facebook (**Figure 5.15**).

Figure 5.15: Pickens Plan highlights its social support.

Implying There Is or There Will Be a Crowd

An infomercial boosted its sales by changing one line of the program from "Operators are waiting. Please call now." to "If operators are busy, please call again."[19] The change suggested that phone lines would be jammed with callers. Along similar lines, Pickens Plan notes that a new corporate partnership is its "first," hinting that more partnerships are to come (**Figure 5.16**).

Figure 5.16: Pickens Plan suggests the first corporate partnership is not the last.

BarackObama.com: Inspiring Hope and Motivating Action

The 2008 U.S. presidential campaign led by Barack Obama marked history for many reasons. One was the campaign website's innovative blend of design, technology, and content. The website communicated the campaign's message and enabled action in ways unlike any other campaign website ever had.

Was the website so effective from day 1? Not exactly. It evolved with help from experts such as Scott Thomas, who served as the campaign's Design Director. When Thomas joined the campaign, he saw opportunity to improve the website.

Thomas explains, "The website was built on the fly as the campaign grew. It was clear to me that the website was like an organism, with content added constantly. Staff were creating pages on a minute-by-minute basis. The site needed a better framework and a more balanced representation of content on the home page."

Consequently, Thomas led a redesign of the campaign website to better organize the content and represent more content on the home page. "We found that people will scroll and explore beyond the top of the screen. At the same time, we kept information on the homepage clear and concise," he notes.

Besides making content easier to find, Thomas sought to inspire people with hope using more than words. He describes the approach this way:

"Obama had laid out his views and his reasons for running in two detailed books. We wanted people who visited the website to feel instantly motivated, so we drew heavily on metaphor, symbolism, and imagery to communicate the campaign's values and messages." (For more detail about the rationale for many of the overall campaign's visual choices, see Thomas' elegant book *Designing Obama*.)

The campaign also shared content and announced events online in innovative ways, such as streaming stump speeches and posting notices on Twitter and Facebook. "Technology is changing the way candidates communicate," says Thomas.

Of course, all the inspiration in the world means little without action. As Thomas explains, "Asking for and supporting offline action was crucial. Presidential campaigns come around only once every four years, so they're the Olympics of campaign technology. We used the latest tools from Blue State Digital to get groups of people together and help them to reach out to others."

People also could donate through the website, which led to an unprecedented number of individual small donations for a presidential campaign and contributed to the campaign's record-breaking fundraising.

No matter your politics, it's clear that BarackObama.com raised the bar of online influence very high.

4. RECIPROCITY: GIVE TO GET

It often involves feeling indebted or obligated to repay a favor.[20] If your neighbor brings you a pie, you likely will feel the need to do something kind for that neighbor in the future. If a week later that same neighbor asks to borrow your drill, you likely will say yes.

Reciprocity is core to business, too. Psychologist Robert Cialdini notes, for example, that "after accepting a gift, customers are willing to purchase products and services they would have otherwise declined."[21]

SIZE AND TIMING MATTER

The larger the favor someone does for you, the more obligated you'll feel for a longer period of time. The sense of obligation for a small gift fades much quicker than that for a large one. If your neighbor who gave you the pie asks a year later to borrow your drill, you might not be as quick to lend it.

TAKING STARTS A SPIRAL OF TAKING

Cialdini focuses much on giving, but reciprocity also applies to taking. If your neighbor lets his dog poo in your yard and later asks to borrow your drill, you likely will say no. And, you might tell your neighbor to buy his own drill and stick it, well, in a certain place. Research suggests that when people experience a snub, they'll retaliate with a more intense rebuke. As University of Chicago professor Boaz Keysar states, "Negative reciprocity, or taking, escalates."[22]

APPLY RECIPROCITY TO CONTENT

Content presents many opportunities to reciprocate and, consequently, build trust or motivate action.

Exchanging Content for Contact Details

A common way to apply reciprocity is to offer visitors useful content and ask for their email address. For example, Content Marketing Institute made a research report freely available and requested contact information in return (**Figure 5.17**).

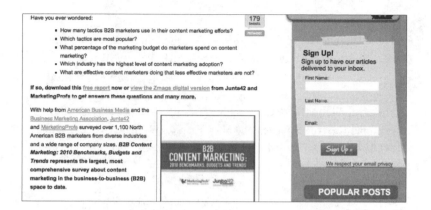

Figure 5.17: Content Marketing Institute offers a free research report and asks for contact details.

Delivering on Brand Promise

When your organization, product, or service delivers what it promises, you're reciprocating your users' money or time. If it doesn't, users will feel taken advantage of and you will run the risk of sparking *a spiral of taking*. Unhappy users might retaliate by posting their complaints to various social networks. If the spiral of taking starts, stop it by giving something—an apology, a discount, something. Learn from United Airlines and its exchange with a musician who felt the airline damaged his guitar. The exchange escalated over the course of a year to the point the musician created a video about the situation. The video went viral, causing United Airlines' stock to plummet overnight (**Figure 5.18**).

Figure 5.18: A musician reciprocated United Airline's treatment of him with a viral video "United Breaks Guitars."

Showing Some Slack

On social networking, people comment or complain about not only products and services but bigger ideas. When that happens, the discussion can be productive or spark the spiral of taking. To keep the discussion productive, show some slack. For example, when a customer asked Frank Eliason, a former representative of Comcast on Twitter (@Comcastcares), about the company's stance on Net neutrality, Frank was not defensive (**Figure 5.19**). Instead, he conceded some points and corrected other points. The result was a respectful discussion.

Figure 5.19:
Frank Eliason
(@ComcastCares)
and Graham
Hill exchanged
concessions about
Net neutrality.

> @comcastcares RE Net neutrality. You will have to take that up with the FCC. They set the rules. Comcast should follow them.
> about 7 hours ago from TweetDeck in reply to comcastcares
>
> @GrahamHill Actually they are not authorized for that by Congress, but hopefully clarification will come
> about 4 hours ago from web in reply to GrahamHill
>
> @comcastcares This is a complex business and moral area. But why is it that no–one trusts telcos/cablecos? Hmmm, I wonder.
> about 7 hours ago from TweetDeck in reply to comcastcares
>
> @GrahamHill I think that goes down to not having more discussion, or pointing to inconsistencies in existing conversations by others.
> about 4 hours ago from web in reply to GrahamHill
>
> @comcastcares You could be right. Plus the actions of a few, like Sprint, give the whole industry a rotten reputation.
> about 6 hours ago from TweetDeck in reply to comcastcares

WHEN TO USE WHAT PRINCIPLES

If Aristotle were around today, I bet he'd tip his hat (or laurel wreath) to modern psychologists. So, let's revisit our guide and add our psychological principles (**Figure 5.20**).

In the first two phases, influencing people's *attitude* is critical. Consider metaphor and framing for content that raises awareness. And, all of these principles can aid your effort to become likable and trusted. To influence *action*, consider the principles of social proof and reciprocity.

	Phase 1 Raise Awareness	Phase 2 Become Liked & Trusted	Phase 3 Motivate, Inspire, & Help Action
RHETORIC			
1A. Credibility	✓	✓	
1B. Logic	✓	✓	✓
1C. Emotion	✓	✓	✓
2. Identification		✓	✓
3. Repetition	✓		✓
4. The Opportune Moment			✓
PSYCHOLOGY			
1. Framing	✓	✓	
2. Metaphor	✓	✓	
3. Social Proof		✓	✓
4. Reciprocity		✓	✓

Figure 5.20: Consider both rhetoric and psychology to make your content influential.

SUMMARY

Psychology is a science with insight into influence; it's not something to rain on our creative parade. These research-based principles complement rhetoric, or the art of influence, to ensure our content gets results. By now, you likely have ideas for applying these principles to your content. To start turning those ideas into plans, press on to Chapter 6.

REFERENCES

1 Merriam-Webster Dictionary at http://www.merriam-webster.com/

2 Jonah Lehrer, *How We Decide* (Hougton Mifflin Harcourt, 2009)

3 Jonah Lehrer, *How We Decide* (Hougton Mifflin Harcourt, 2009)

4 Scott London, How the Media Frames Political Issues at http://www.scottlondon.com/reports/frames.html

5 Susan D. Moeller, Considering the Media's Framing and Agenda-Setting Roles in States' Responsiveness to Natural Crises and Disasters, *Harvard Business Review*

6 Richard H. Thaler, *Nudge* (Yale University Press, 2008)

7 Richard H. Thaler, *Nudge* (Yale University Press, 2008)

8 Jennifer Van Grove, How Starbucks Plans to Capitalize on Free Wi-Fi at http://mashable.com/2010/08/12/starbucks-digital-network/

9 Pickens Plan – The Plan at http://www.pickensplan.com/theplan/

10 Colleen Jones, Kevin O'Connor, Testing Content at
http://www.slideshare.net/leenjones/content-testing-early-often-well

11 Shakespeare, Sonnet 18

12 Steven Pinker, *The Stuff of Thought* (Viking, 2007)

13 Gerald Zaltman, Lindsay Zaltman, *Marketing Metaphoria* (Harvard Business School
Press, 2008)

14 Dan Saffer, The Role of Metaphor in Interaction Design at
http://www.slideshare.net/dansaffer/the-role-of-metaphor-in-interaction-design

15 Method – our story at http://methodhome.com/methodology/our-story

16 Robert Cialdini, *Influence: The Psychology of Persuasion* (Collins, 1998)

17 Richard H. Thaler, *Nudge* (Yale University Press, 2008)

18 Richard H. Thaler, *Nudge* (Yale University Press, 2008)

19 Noah J. Goldstein, Steve J. Martin, Robert Cialdini, *Yes! 50 Scientifically Proven Ways to Be
Persuasive* (Free Press, 2008)

20 Robert Cialdini, *Influence: The Psychology of Persuasion* (Collins, 1998)

21 Robert Cialdini, *Influence: The Psychology of Persuasion* (Collins, 1998)

22 Boaz Keysar, Benjamin A. Converse, Jiunwen Wang, Nicholas Epley, Reciprocity is Not
Give and Take: Asymmetric Reciprocity to Positive and Negative Acts at
http://news.uchicago.edu/images/pdf/081217.GiveTake.pdf

THE CLIMB

Knowing principles is one thing. Applying them is another thing—actually, a list of things. (I *did* say it's a harder road!) Plan your route to clout with the right questions and tools. Evaluate your progress with the right data. And, heed ethics along the way.

6 PLAN

• •

You've seen the principles. Now, you're ready to start the climb to clout. That takes time and effort. To get a head start, ask the right questions and let the answers guide your planning. Learn more about considerations and tools for your journey.

I ARISE IN THE MORNING TORN BETWEEN A DESIRE TO IMPROVE THE WORLD AND A DESIRE TO ENJOY THE WORLD. THIS MAKES IT HARD TO PLAN THE DAY.

—E. B. White, author

To influence what users think *and* do, your website content requires careful planning. But, even the planning can be hard.

THE PLANNING PREDICAMENT

A website and its content used to be pretty simple. A few years ago, a website focused on either what people thought (attitude) or what they did (action). A marketing website was a brochure. A media website was a newspaper or magazine. An e-commerce website was a catalog and cash register. A service website tracked our monthly statements and took our payments. A web forum was our social connection. The content for each type of website followed suit.

Now, to make life simpler for our users, our websites are becoming much more complex. Our websites are no longer either magazines or product catalogs or marketing brochures or self-service stations or forums. Our websites are becoming all of those things *at once*. And, our websites are becoming connected to social networks. As a result, our websites are starting to merge all of that content and data together. Our websites are evolving into complex mashups.

This seismic change is very good. Why? Because now a website—and its content—can influence what users think *and* what users do. A website can help a user make a decision and act on it better than ever before.

Take the hugely popular Mint.com, for example. Aaron Patzer started it because he spent a long Saturday afternoon trying to answer a basic question: How much money did he spend and save that month?[1] After toggling between his accounts at bank, credit card, and investment websites, he still couldn't get a clear answer. He decided to change that by bringing together all of the content and data a user needs to make budget decisions. The result is Mint, which assembles editorial content, marketing content, personal finance data, user-generated content (UGC), and support content (**Figure 6.1**).

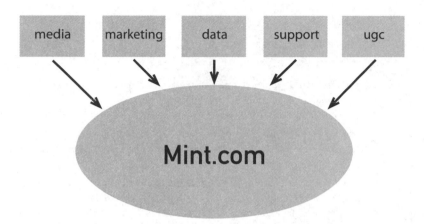

Figure 6.1: Mint.com mashes up data and content to influence financial decisions.

This blend of content and data addresses what users think and what they do, as shown in **Table 6.1**. People use Mint to stay aware of their budget, change their spending habits, and reach financial goals.[2] That's powerful clout.

Table 6.1: Mint.com Tackles What Users Think *and* Do

CONTENT FOR ATTITUDE	CONTENT AND DATA FOR ACTION
Marketing (why and how sign up)	Data (dashboard and reminders)
Media (blog articles)	Marketing (product suggestions)
UGC (blog comments)	Support

Mint is only one example of our websites' potential to influence. Although bringing all this data and content together is good for users, it wreaks havoc on many organizations' approach toward content. Large organizations tend to plan for content in silos and then have a mess when the content merges together.[3] Small organizations tend not to plan for it at all. And, anyone dealing with web content can become overwhelmed with the many content options. To bring your website to its full potential, plan to integrate the right content in the right way.

Retail and Media Merge Content—and Business Models

What if your clothing retailer was your source for fashion trends and advice? What if you could instantly buy that cool bauble featured in your favorite design magazine? What if you could earn points for reading your favorite tech magazine, then redeem those points for discounts on gadgets?

As the way we use websites evolves, businesses are mashing up. A particularly juicy melding of models is retail and media: as the *Wall Street Journal* has observed.[4] Shopping and consuming editorial content blend into one online experience.

For example, I advised FootSmart, a lower-body health retailer, in planning to add niche editorial content to its e-commerce website. FootSmart CEO Alan Beychok explains why he wanted to expand into media: "My vision for FootSmart is to be our customers' complete outfitter for lower-body health. When customers turn to us, we want to be easy to find and ready to advise. Quality editorial content will reinforce our brand positioning and help us make that vision a reality."

FootSmart CMO Trish Tobin adds, "We are building a strong community of customers on Facebook by answering questions in a direct and authentic way, giving advice, and encouraging other customers to chime in with their own experiences. Editorial content like this will bridge our social presence with our product content."

It's not hard to imagine this trend expanding to other industries. Watch it closely.

THE ANSWER? SIX KEY QUESTIONS

To make your content more influential, take a holistic approach to planning. Let your guide be your answers to the five Ws and H:

- *Why* are you influencing a result with content?
- *What* content in what style will influence the result?
- *Who* will be the influencer?
- *Where* will you influence with content?
- *When* will you influence with content?
- *How* will you get, create, and maintain the influential content?

Understanding context is critical to answering these questions. In fact, most of these questions fit the elements of context we discussed in Chapter 3 (**Figure 6.2**).

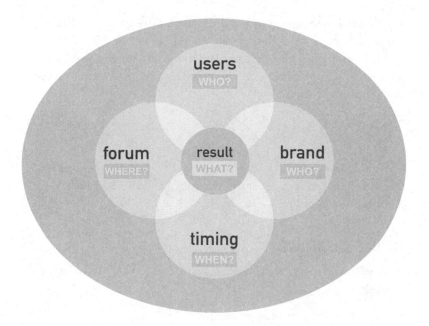

Figure 6.2: Planning questions address the elements of context.

Let's look at each question and how to answer it with principles and tools.

WHY?

You'll know *why* if you've gone through the content strategy process (see the Strategy section in Chapter 2). If not, think about it now. Why are you striving for the result you want? Does that fit your business or organization goals and priorities?

The answer will guide your answers to the rest of these questions and prioritize your content decisions. For example, when I worked with the online retailer FootSmart on a strategic plan for their web content, we discussed *why* at length. The answer? FootSmart wanted to be the ultimate outfitter for foot and lower-body health. The CEO and CMO viewed influential web content as the best way to guide, or outfit, customers in their buying decisions. That's a good answer because it ties content to business results and user needs.

What would be a bad answer? The retailer wants to start a blog to keep pace with the times. That's bad because it doesn't connect content, business results, and user needs. The answer also specifies where the content will be (in a blog) before you've had a chance to consider the options.

So, after you have a good grasp on why, you can move on to the other questions. I'm presenting these questions in the order I find most helpful. In reality, these questions depend on each other. You likely will think about many of them at the same time and adjust your answers as you plan. That's perfectly OK.

WHAT?

In thinking about *what,* you're deciding on the *substance* of your content, especially its meaning and style, to get results. Consider these questions, principles, and tools.

GUIDING QUESTIONS

What will make your content's meaning and style influential to your users? Think about

- What should you say through content?
- What evidence supports what you want to say?
- What is the best way to say it, including the best tone, style, and theme?

PERTINENT PRINCIPLES

To help you answer these questions, draw on your understanding of the users and brand as discussed in Chapter 3. Also consider these principles from rhetoric and psychology discussed in Chapters 4 and 5:

- Emotion
- Logic
- Framing
- Metaphor

Emotion, logic, and framing will help you decide what to say, choose supporting evidence, and consider variations for each phase. Emotion and metaphor will inspire the tone, style, and theme.

HANDY TOOLS

To document your decisions, use a message architecture and an editorial style guide.

Message Architecture

A message architecture captures the essence of what you want to say. It documents your key messages (or claims), aligns them with your brand values, and ensures they resonate with the users you want to reach.

Support your key messages with facts and examples (sometimes called proof points). You might not use that evidence in all of your content, but that evidence ensures your messages are based on truth and guarantees you can deliver what the messages promise.

> **REVEAL, DON'T REPEAT**
>
> Don't blast key messages over and over. Instead, let content reveal and support different facets of the messages.

Also, start developing your brand's voice. Infuse it with appropriate tone and emotion. The voice makes your content special and easier to remember. **Figure 6.3** shows a sample message architecture for a shoe retailer that specializes in foot health.

Figure 6.3: This sample message architecture ties claims to evidence.

MESSAGE CHECK

Find out whether your messages and voice are on the right path. Test them with users. (See Chapter 8.)

Editorial Style Guide

Capture your message architecture, details of your brand voice, word usage, and other standards in a style guide. The guide will help you preserve your unique style over time and across many authors, personas, or content creators. For a beautiful and useful example of an editorial style guide, see *The Yahoo! Style Guide* and its website (styleguide.yahoo.com).

Include social considerations in your style guide. For example, the USA.gov style guide includes clear examples of dos and don'ts for sharing content on Twitter and Facebook (**Figure 6.4**).

Figure 6.4: USA.gov explains style guidelines for sharing content on Facebook.

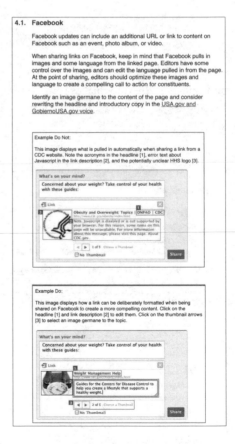

WHO?

Identify the people to represent or associate with your brand. Decide *who* will contribute content on your website, share your content on social networking, endorse you, or otherwise be your online personality.

GUIDING QUESTIONS

Who can best represent your brand? Who can attract the right users and interact with them well? Consider

- What personality characteristics fit your brand values and voice?
- What personality characteristics suit the role? Should the personality that provides customer care be different from the personality that supports a campaign?
- Who is a trusted authority and good communicator about topics relevant to your brand?
- What personality or organization would be a credible endorsement?
- Who will respond in a crisis?

PERTINENT PRINCIPLES

As you think about your answers, consider these principles from rhetoric and psychology discussed in Chapters 4 and 5:

- Credibility
- Identification
- Reciprocity
- Social proof

Credibility and identification will help you choose personalities and endorsements that resonate with your users. Reciprocity and social proof help guide your personalities' interactions.

HANDY TOOLS

To capture your decisions, define a brand persona and note it in your editorial style guide.

Brand Persona

A brand persona summarizes the personality characteristics and role that you want the personality to play. For example, **Figure 6.5** shows how a shoe retailer might define three personas:

- A lively host persona inspired by Joy Behar, who shares similar demographics with most of the website's users, for blog posts and podcasts.

- A podiatrist as a health expert persona for guest editorial content and occasional blog or podcast interviews.

- A style expert persona for product picks and occasional blog or podcast interviews.

For initial planning, even a few statements and pictures of your sources of inspiration will help you think through personas (Figure 6.5).

Figure 6.5: A sample plan for personas

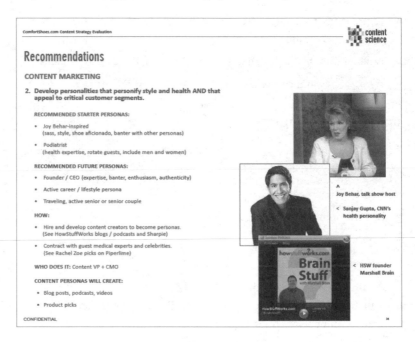

Editorial Style Guide

List your personas and any exceptions or additions to the style guide for your personas. For example, the shoe retailer would not want the host persona to speak in the same style as a podiatrist.

Also, note who will speak in an emergency or crisis situation. Usually, your best bet is for the head of your organization to respond.

WHERE?

Decide on your content's *form*, *location*, and *display*.

GUIDING QUESTIONS

Where will your content best influence? Consider where your users will access it and these questions:

- In what format will your content best influence attitude and action?
- Where (on what forums) will users best find and use your content?
- Where should content be on your website and in your web pages to support attitude and action?

PERTINENT PRINCIPLES

These principles are useful in contemplating where your content will influence:

- Credibility
- Emotion
- Logic
- Reciprocity
- Social proof

Credibility, emotion, and logic will help you pick appropriate content formats. Reciprocity and social proof will aid some decisions about where to put the content.

HANDY FORMATS AND TOOLS

First, let's talk about content formats, then we'll look at several tools.

Content Formats

Formats are where your content comes to life, so choose them wisely. Text (words) always has been and always will be a critical content format for our websites. In the past, words also were practical because they worked well for users with slow Internet connections. Today, many users have faster connections, so we can realistically consider other formats for our websites. It's also much easier today to produce and distribute a variety of content formats. So, we have more content options than ever.

As you plan, consider that different formats work well for different aspects of influence. Some formats showcase personality so that users identify with you. Others work well for presenting a logical argument or evidence so that users trust you. Let's take a closer look at these basic formats.

> **MORE ISN'T ALWAYS BETTER**
> Don't create a lot of content just because you can.
> Start small, go for high quality, and then grow.

Text

Words support every aspect of influence. Words are ideal to make a case, communicate an opinion, or sustain a complex argument. Words help convey key messages and reinforce themes. Text also tells stories, conveys personality, and injects emotion into a story or call to action. And words instruct clearly.

It's also easy to find words on the web. Search engines still work best with words. Text in the form of metadata can help you make other content formats easier for search engines to find. Words drive much social networking, such as status updates. Words are the lifeblood of your content.

Podcasts/Audio

Audio is ideal for people who speak well. Audio does much of the same work that words do. In addition, audio can showcase interactions, such as interesting interviews or friendly banter (**Figure 6.6**).

Podcasts distribute simply through RSS (really simple syndication) feeds, too.

Figure 6.6: ESPN offers a banter-filled Fantasy Football podcast.

Images

Photos and images, especially those with compelling visuals, tell stories. Profile photos identify people, reinforcing their credibility and showing their personality. Photos also tap into people's emotions and show sensory detail to cause visceral reactions (**Figure 6.7**). As well, photos help instruct by showing how to take an action.

Figure 6.7: A large, detailed photo of a cheeseburger might make a carnivore's mouth water.

How can you make photos and images easier for people to find through search and social networking? Distribute photos through Flickr.com. You can easily create different groupings of photos and feed them to your website or social networks. And, you can tag the photos using search-friendly words.

Videos

Use videos to showcase people or personas with a lot of presence. Videos also tell stories well. Streaming video allows you to share an event live, as it's happening. And, videos are ideal for explaining how to do something (**Figure 6.8**).

Figure 6.8: A video from Williams-Sonoma explains how to prepare a gourmet dish to someone culinarily challenged, like me

A useful way to distribute videos is through YouTube.com. Once you place a video there, you can embed it on your website or on social networks. Your users can share the love and embed it, too. And, you can describe the video in words that search engines find easily. (It doesn't hurt that Google owns YouTube, too.)

Slides

Slides are the artifacts of a presentation. They're useful to show the outline and key points of an argument with words and visuals (**Figure 6.9**). Slides also can explain how to do something.

You can distribute slides easily through Slideshare.net. Similar to Flickr and YouTube, you can post your slide sets and then embed them on your website and on social networks. And, you can add descriptive words that make your slides easy to find through search engines.

Figure 6.9: Using slides to explain content analysis.

Data Visualizations

If you need to make a point grounded in research, consider how to visualize that point. A data visualization can simply be an image (**Figure 6.10**), or it can be more interactive and animated.

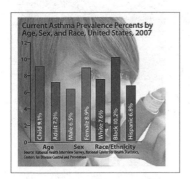

Figure 6.10: Centers for Disease Control and Prevention provide a simple visual of some data.

Whitepapers, E-books, and Reports

Book-inspired content works well for telling a longer story or making a detailed case. It's also useful for in-depth instruction. This content is most commonly offered in PDF (portable document format) or a proprietary e-book format.

If you're freely distributing this content or a sample of it, consider uploading your PDF to Issu.com, which works similarly to Slideshare and Flickr (**Figure 6.11**).

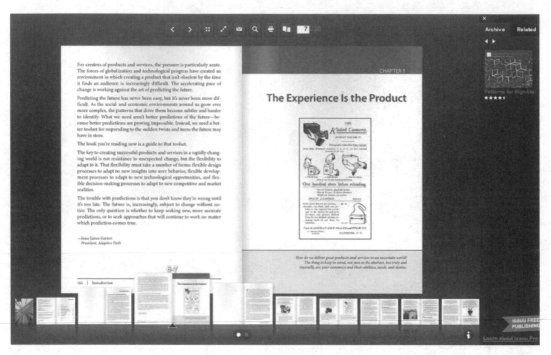

Figure 6.11: Adaptive Path offers a book sample on issu.com.

To boost your planning, **Table 6.2** summarizes the influential ways to use and distribute content formats other than words. To learn about modeling content, see the How section in this chapter.

Table 6.2: Influencing with Content Formats (Other Than Text)

FORMAT	WORKS REALLY WELL FOR...	DISTRIBUTES EASILY WITH...
Audio	Personality, stories	RSS feeds, iTunes
Images	Visual stories, sensory detail, instruction	Flickr.com
Video	Stories, personality, live events, instruction	YouTube.com
Slides	Cases, instruction	Slideshare.net
Data Visualizations	Evidence for cases	Flickr.com (if it's an image)
Whitepapers, E-books, Reports	Stories, Cases, Instruction	Issuu.com

Concept Model

We've zoomed into details of content types and formats. Now, let's zoom out to the big picture of where your content will go on your website and beyond. Enter the concept model.

A concept model will help you and your stakeholders keep your *entire content ecosystem*, not just your website, in mind. A concept model shows

- The connection between your content and the ways users become aware of your content, such as social networks, search results, and email.
- A high-level organization of content.
- The connection between your different categories or types of content.

This model conveys at a glance how vast and interdependent most content efforts are. For example, **Figure 6.12** is a concept model for an online retailer in the health industry. It represents content about the products, content about health topics, search engine marketing content, and media content. Is that all? Nope. It also shows the basic connection to search, social networking, and email.

LETTING GO OF THE HOME PAGE

People find your content in many ways other than your website's home page. That means your deeper content is as important for influence as your home page.

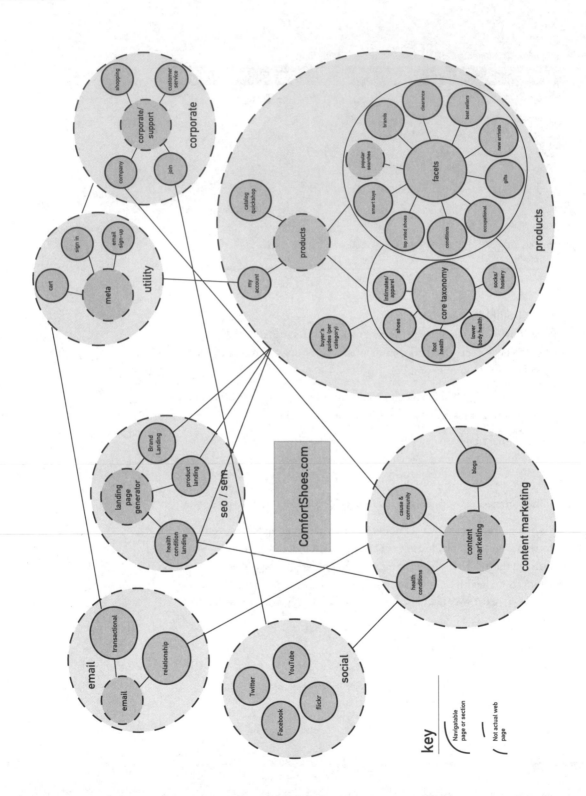

The model will help you plan the big picture of where, and communicate it to executives and stakeholders. That's very handy when you need to ask for more time or resources to support your content plans.

Content Matrix

A content matrix is a spreadsheet that documents in more detail what content formats and types you have and, ultimately, where they will go (**Figure 6.13**). For a useful explanation and a sample matrix spreadsheet, see *The Web Content Strategist's Bible*. Your matrix should be in lockstep with your site map (see Other Handy Tools).

Figure 6.12 (opposite): This concept model for an online retailer shows the connection between search, social networking, and other web content.

Search and Social Networks: The Gateways to Your Content

Where do users start in their quest for web content? For a while, the main gateways to the Internet were portals, such as Yahoo! and AOL. Then, for years, keyword search, especially Google, was the main gateway. Now, social networks are emerging as a gateway.[5] Which ones should you plan for?

While portals might remain important publishers, I predict portals will keep declining as a gateway to the Internet. Portals offer too much content about too many topics from too many brands and authors. Portals can become more relevant to users if users set their profiles, but that's a lot of work for the user. Portals can become more relevant by remembering user behavior (such as what topics a user visits), too, but that takes a while. The user has to visit and remain on the portal at least a few times.

Social networking compensates for many drawbacks of portals. When someone's friends and colleagues share content, it's more likely to be relevant. Those friends and colleagues act like personal content curators. So, creating or being mentioned in content that the right people will share is important to your effort.

Search will continue to be valuable when people know specifically what they want. Search is evolving. Bing, a semantic search engine, has arrived on the scene. Google continues to add features such as instant search, which immediately updates search results *while* a user types keywords. So, ensure your content appears in search results for pertinent key words through good (not snake oil) search engine optimization.

For an introduction to using keywords in your content, see *The Web Content Strategist's Bible* by Richard Sheffield. For a detailed look at developing quality content for keyword search, see *Audience, Relevance, and Search* by James Mathewson, Frank Donatone, and Cynthia Fishel.

Figure 6.13: A matrix tracks your content types and formats in detail.

	A	B	C	D	E	F
1	ComfortShoes.com Content Matrix					
2						
3	Page ID	Page/Section Name	Author	Notes/Comments	Existing URL	SEO Keywords
124	2.8.1.0	Women's Sandals			www.comfortshoes.com/womensshoes/sandals.html	shoes, women, women's, sandals
125	2.8.2.0	Women's Slippers			www.comfortshoes.com/womensshoes/slippers.html	shoes, women, women's, slippers
126	2.8.3.0	Women's Shoe Aids / Accessories			www.comfortshoes.com/womensshoes/shoeaids.html	shoes, women, women's, shoe aids, accessories
127	2.8.4.0	Women's New Arrivals		Updated monthly	www.comfortshoes.com/womensshoes/newarrivals.htm	shoes, women, women's, new, newest
128	2.8.5.0	Women's Top Brands		Error on Page – Content Missing	www.comfortshoes.com/womensshoes/topbrands.html	shoes, women, women's, brands, top, best
129	2.8.6.0	Women's Best Sellers		Updated monthly	www.comfortshoes.com/womensshoes/bestsellers.html	shoes, women, women's, best selling, best selle
130	**2.9.0.0**	**Men's Shoes**		**Note Men's Sandals was not a functioning page and has been removed.**	www.comfortshoes.com/mensshoes/index.html	**shoes, men, men's, slippers, shoe aids, accessories, new, top, best, brands**
131	2.9.1.0	Men's Slippers			www.comfortshoes.com/mensshoes/slippers.html	shoes, men, men's, slippers
132	2.9.1.1	Men's Shoe Aids / Accessories			www.comfortshoes.com/mensshoes/shoeaids.html	shoes, men, men's, shoe aids, accessories
133	2.9.1.2	Men's New Arrivals		Updated monthly	www.comfortshoes.com/mensshoes/newarrivals.html	shoes, men, men's, new, newest
134	2.9.1.3	Men's Top Brands			www.comfortshoes.com/mensshoes/topbrands.html	shoes, men, men's top, brands, best
135	2.9.1.4	Men's Best Sellers		Updated monthly	www.comfortshoes.com/mensshoes/bestsellers.html	shoes, men, men's,best selling, best sellers
136	**2.10.0.0**	**Top Rated Shoes**	**CPJ**		www.comfortshoes.com/toprated/index.html	**shoes, men, women, best, top rated**
137	2.10.1.0	Top Rated Men's Shoe's			www.comfortshoes.com/toprated/mens.html	shoes, men, men's, top rated, best
138	2.10.1.1	Top Rated Women's Shoes			www.comfortshoes.com/toprated/womens.html	shoes, women, women's, top rated, best
139	**2.11.0.0**	**Smart Buys**	**CPJ**	**See subpages for content to tease on this page. Use Top Rated wireframe.**	www.comfortshoes.com/smartbuys/index.html	shoes, men, women, smart buys, best, sales
140	**2.12.0.0**	**Clearance**	**CPJ**	**Need consensus on how often this is updated; not clear from background**	www.comfortshoes.com/clearance/index.html	**shoes, men, women, clearance, sales**
141	2.12.1.0	Socks			www.comfortshoes.com/clearance/socks.html	shoes, men, women, clearance, socks
142	2.12.2.0	Health		Error on Page – Content Missing	www.comfortshoes.com/clearance/health.html	shoes, men, women, clearance, health
143	**2.13.0.0**	**Support**	**CPJ**		www.comfortshoes.com/support/index.html	
144	2.13.1.0	Forgot Password?			www.comfortshoes.com/support/password.html	

Copy Deck

A copy deck (sometimes called a page table) includes your writing or text content as well as other types of text, such as interface labels, page titles, and metadata. The copy deck helps specify the *form* your words will take. Where will you use paragraphs, headings, bulleted lists, or numbered steps? When do you need a table? These are just some of the questions that a copy deck helps answer about form. The definitive guide on writing in the best form for the web is *Letting Go of the Words*.

Other Handy Tools

Deciding where your content should go relates to information architecture. Information architecture helps *structure* and *organize* content. So, you'll find some information architecture tools useful, including

- Site map, which specifies the pages and screens and how they're organized
- Wireframes of page or screen templates

If you don't actually create these documents, you'll want to review and provide feedback on them. You want to ensure that structure, form, and content work together rather than fight each other. For a detailed guide through many of these tools, see *Communicating Design* by Dan Brown. For advice on how content strategists, information architects, and designers can collaborate, see *Content Strategy for the Web*.

WHEN?

For your content to influence people, you need to ensure the right content gets to the right users at the right time. Think about the content *timing* and *business logic*.

GUIDING QUESTIONS

When will your content influence? Consider questions such as

- When will you create, publish, and archive content?
- When will you emphasize or discuss what topics, themes, or messages appear in your content?
- When will you make dynamic content (such as a reminder) display?
- When should users have access or not have access to certain content?

PERTINENT PRINCIPLES

Consider these principles related to timing:

- Repetition
- The opportune moment

Repetition will help you identify hooks and plan themes. The opportune moment will help ensure you're prepared for key moments of influence, such as the call to act or a crisis response.

HANDY TOOLS

For planning issues around when, use the content lifecycle, the editorial calendar, and business rules and requirements.

Content Lifecycle (Shelf Life)

This tool summarizes the life of all your content, from when you create it to when you archive it. It specifies your content's shelf life. Just as an apple goes bad much quicker than a block of cheese, different sets of content can have different shelf lives. For example, a video for a campaign should expire sooner than content about your core product or service (**Figure 6.14**).

Figure 6.14: Different content requires different timing of the life cycle.

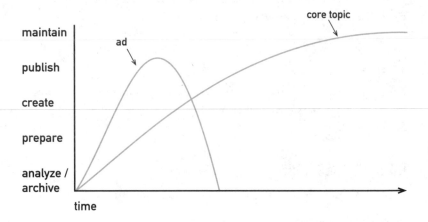

There isn't a single correct life cycle—content experts argue it has anywhere from three to fifteen phases. *You* have to define what phases make sense for your content and, most importantly, the *timing* of those phases. To give you a head start, consider these phases:

- *Analyze* your situation for the content you need.
- *Create* or *collect* the content.
- *Publish* the content.
- *Archive* the content.

The best benefit to planning the lifecycle is it helps *everyone*—from IT to marketing—know what to expect and schedule their workload accordingly. The lifecycle also allows you to take advantage of the automation that a content management system (CMS) offers, such as automatically archiving your content at a certain date or after a certain length of time.

Editorial or Conversation Calendar

As I noted in Chapter 4, an editorial calendar helps you plan what content to create over time so you don't repeat yourself. It also prevents you from scrambling for content ideas or being surprised by new content needs. The editorial calendar is inspired by the publishing industry (**Figure 6.15**).

EDITORIAL CALENDAR

ISSUE	CLOSING DATE	ON-SALE DATE	EDITORIAL CONTENT
February	12/10/10	1/18/11	The Creative Economy New ideas to drive fresh thinking in business, government, and your career
March*	1/13/11	2/22/11	Most Innovative Companies 2011 Annual ranking of the best in business, across industries and across the globe
April	2/17/11	3/29/11	The New Rules of Leadership From mavericks to mentors, defining leadership in today's business landscape
May	3/17/11	4/26/11	Fast Cities Hot spots of business and culture
June*	4/14/11	5/24/11	The 100 Most Creative People in Business Dazzling thinkers, rising stars, and boldfaced names reshaping the future
July/August	5/19/11	6/28/11	Shaking Up the Future of Marketing Lessons from the coolest companies around
September	7/07/11	8/16/11	Green Revolution Sustainable solutions from unexpected places

Figure 6.15: Fast Company offers a glimpse at its editorial calendar.

This calendar is appropriate for editorial content, such as articles or blog posts, and social network/media content. Use it to plan

- Fresh perspectives on or updates for core topics.
- Campaigns, promotions, and causes.
- News, announcements, and features.
- Topics and conversation arcs for social networking.

To get the most value out of your calendar, track elements such as

- Topic
- Author and editor
- Dates to start and finish creating the content
- Date to publish content
- Where to publish the content (website, social networking, email, and so on)

You get out of this tool what you put into it. If you and your team don't keep it updated, it won't help you. Start with a simple calendar in a spreadsheet that's easy to maintain. As you grow, you can add more detail.

> **EMERGING TOOLS**
>
> A WordPress plug-in called Editorial Calendar is now available. Editorial strategist Jeffrey MacIntyre predicts more database-driven calendars, too.

Business Rules and Requirements

When should a user get a reminder or a suggestion? When should a user see a special promotion or advertisement? Should some users have access only to certain content? Answers to questions likes these lie in business rules and requirements for your content. Devote time to thinking through them carefully so you can use the power of technology wisely.

Business rules are statements that define what can or cannot be done. They're based on business goals and processes. Here's an example:

We must remind the user of a health appointment three business days ahead of the appointment.

Business requirements define how to follow the rule on your website. For example, a basic requirement based on the rule above might be

Three business days before a health appointment, the system will display a reminder message on the website and send a text message.

A business analyst can help you document rules and requirements, but you and your team must contribute significantly to defining them. They are not just a bunch of words on paper or buried in a prototype. They are the *only* way to ensure your website content works as you intend and to plan for all the right variations of your content types and templates.

Look After Your Business Logic

. . . .

Keep track of your rules and requirements after your redesign, new design, or other web project is done. More than once, I've walked into a project for a large existing website, and no one knows exactly how the site works. No one can completely explain the logic that drives what content users see and when. To figure it out, my team or I spend time experimenting with the site and piecing together clues from different people who worked on it.

All that time could have been saved if someone maintained that logic.

I recently talked about this bad habit of overlooking logic with Shelly Bowen, principal of the content strategy firm Pybop. She sums up why it happens well:

"Many companies begin with only one or a few content contributors, so it's easy to communicate and keep an eye on the logic that plays out. When the company grows and content builds in volume and complexity, processes aren't in place to pass along the business rules and requirements. New projects may establish rules that override or conflict with currently playing logic, or the rules may not incorporate valuable insights from past projects' successes and mishaps."

So, put someone—or some people—in charge of tracking your business logic. Also, use caution before making your business rules—and consequently, the development logic—very complicated. The more complicated the logic, the harder it will be to keep track of, and the more carefully you'll need to think through new projects that might affect the logic.

HOW?

Decide *how* you will make your influential content happen. You'll need to think in more detail about your content processes, methods, and other behind-the-scenes aspects of your website.

GUIDING QUESTIONS

How will you get, create, and maintain the influential content?

PERTINENT PRINCIPLES

The key principle for how is credibility. Ensure you can maintain quality content, use quality sources, and employ ethical methods so your brand remains credible to your users. (For more about ethics, see Chapter 11.)

HANDY ACTIVITIES

Planning for how is more about activities than tools. You need to do a lot to make content happen. If you've already thought about content strategy and creating quality content, then you're already exploring some of these activities.

Creating and Sourcing Content

Figure out what content you will create and what content you will source. Your exact plan for how will depend on your specific situation, but these questions will help you think through it.

Will you create some or all of your content? If so

- Do you have all the right people, from writers to copyeditors to photographers to videographers to managing editors to producers?
- Will those people be in-house, freelance, outsourced, or a combination? Who will manage your content creation?
- What workflow will you use to create the content? Who will approve what and when?

Will you mash up content and data from different sources? If so

- How will you get the content and data and bring it together?
- How will your development team help?

Will you use syndicated or licensed content? If so

- Can you afford to buy it?
- Have you followed all the proper policies and legalities with the sources and your own organization?
- Can your development team use and parse the feeds?

Will you curate or repackage content from your archives, from other sources, or from users? If so

- How will you coordinate it with your editorial efforts? What will be the theme or occasion for curating or repackaging?
- Do you need permissions or approvals to curate content from other sources? Are you giving proper attribution to the content sources?

- Have you set clear expectations with users about when and how you will curate their content? Is your approach to curating user-generated content reflected in your privacy policy?

  CLASHING ETHICS

  Social media enthusiasts, publishers, and marketers can have conflicting views of ethics—when is it free to share, and when is it not? Learn more in Chapter 11.

Modeling Content Types and Templates

Define your content types and how your content types should fit into templates. Modeling content types is critical if your website uses a CMS. Modeling makes your content as flexible and manageable as possible. If you're not using a CMS, you'll still like modeling content types and templates. The process helps you (or your team) think through how to structure your content in detail. This planning helps designers and developers build templates that actually fit your web content.

Modeling content types can get extremely detailed, so I'm going to show one example. Ideally, you would have content types to address all the content on your website and all the ways you want to use that content. To learn more about modeling content types, see the *Content Management Bible* by Bob Boiko.

Let's say to build trust with your users, you plan to have credible articles about pertinent topics on your website. For instance, American Express OPEN Forum offers a website for small businesses with articles about innovation, marketing, finance, and more. You can plan an *article* content type by modeling its structure. To model it, include the obvious stuff that you would see on a web page such as

- Title
- Summary
- Author name
- Author bio
- Author image
- Date published
- Body text
- Image

You can get very detailed for each element, such as specifying character lengths or date formats. Also include less obvious administrative stuff that will help you organize the content such as

- Topic(s)
- Date created
- Editor

When you model the content this way, you make it easier to organize, easier to maintain, and easier to present in different ways on your website. One of the most important benefits is presenting several content types together in a template.

Here's an example. You can combine a well-modeled article type with other content types that have something in common, such as topic. Then, you can create a topic template that serves as a search-friendly gateway to all your content types and formats about that topic. For instance, OPEN Forum offers an Innovation gateway page that combines articles, video, and more (**Figure 6.16**).

Figure 6.16: The topic index page compiles a variety of topic content types.

Governing Content

As your follow your plan, you might need to make changes to how you create and source content, how you define workflow, how you model content, and more. Governance defines a process for how you will decide about those changes. Who will be involved? How often will changes be considered? Who has the final say? For an excellent discussion of governance, see *Content Strategy for the Web* by Kristina Halvorson.

THE CONTENT BRIEF: YOUR ANSWERS AT A GLANCE

The content brief is your master plan. It summarizes the answers to your key questions, making the path for your journey clear. Whether you're with a large organization, a small business, or on your own, you'll find the content brief handy for

- Giving yourself and your team a vision for influencing through content.
- Communicating your vision to executives, stakeholders, clients, or new content contributors.

The essence of your content brief is the five Ws and H—but customize it as you see fit (**Figure 6.17**). With this brief in hand, you're well on your way to turning your content into a source of clout.

ComfortShoes.com Content Strategy Evaluation — content science

Content Brief: ComfortShoes.com

WHY?

ComfortShoes.com wants to bring its niche brand to life through content that

- Shows values that users will like and trust.
- Helps users select the right shoes.
- Gives users reasons to return to ComfortShoes.com.

WHO?

ComfortShoes.com will speak as a brand and add three important personas to its blog and social networking:

- Host persona.
- Podiatrist (health expert persona).
- Style expert persona.

WHEN?

This effort requires content that changes more often than ComfortShoes.com's content for its products.

ComfortShoes.com will rely heavily on its editorial calendar to schedule content topics and themes across the blog and social networking.

WHAT?

ComfortShoes.com will

- Support its updated key messages.
- Speak consistently in a credible, friendly voice.
- Follow a new editorial style guide.

WHERE?

ComfortShoes.com will enhance its community on Facebook, revamp its blog, and add these content formats:

- Video of a podiatrist explaining foot conditions and how comfort shoes help.
- Podcasts of the host persona interviewing the expert personas and occasional guests.

HOW?

ComfortShoes.com will hire a content producer to lead a team of in-house and freelance content contributors and govern content policies.

The content producer will work in lock step with the Chief Marketing Officer.

Figure 6.17: The content brief acts as your trail guide on the climb to clout.

SUMMARY

To achieve clout, you need a holistic plan to make your content influential. That plan depends on your answers to the 5 Ws and H:

- *Why* are you influencing a result with content?

- *What* content in what style will influence the result?

- *Who* will be the influencer?

- *Where* will you influence with content?

- *When* will you influence with content?

- *How* will you get, create, and maintain the influential content?

As you climb this higher road, you'll hit roadblocks. (I warned this road was harder!) But, don't give up. Persist. Learn more in Chapter 7.

REFERENCES

1 Mint Founder on Branding: Keep It Simple at http://news.cnet.com/8301-13577_3-10457870-36.html

2 Andy Greenberg, Making a Mint at http://www.forbes.com/2008/01/03/microsoft-google-intuit-tech-ebiz-cx_ag_0103mint.html

3 Ann Rockley, *Managing Enterprise Content* (New Riders, 2002)

4 Geoffrey A. Fowler, Jessica E. Vascellaro, Media and Retail Firms Meld Business Models Online at http://online.wsj.com/article/SB10001424052748703620604575348973109834894.html

5 Jon Gibs, Social Media: The Next Great Gateway for Content Discovery? at http://blog.nielsen.com/nielsenwire/online_mobile/social-media-the-next-great-gateway-for-content-discovery/

7 PERSIST THROUGH ROADBLOCKS

· ·

As you climb the higher and harder road to clout, you'll hit a roadblock (or a roadblock will hit you). Overcome common obstacles with help from these tips and examples.

EVERYONE HAS A PLAN 'TIL THEY GET PUNCHED IN THE MOUTH.

—Mike Tyson, championship boxer

Even with the best plans, you might face a barrier (or several) on your climb to clout. Don't give up. You'll prevail with a lot of persistence and a little help from insight based on my many years in the trenches.

For your journey, let's take a look at some challenges and how to overcome them. You might face

- Roadblocks before launch
- Roadblocks while raising awareness
- Roadblocks while becoming liked and trusted
- Roadblocks while inspiring, motivating, and helping action

ROADBLOCKS BEFORE LAUNCH

Some roadblocks can stop you before you even start, such as

- Starting with nothing
- Starting with an intranet landfill

STARTING WITH NOTHING

You have little content and few resources. Where should you focus? Here's my advice for startups and small businesses.

Disruptive Startup

You're shaking things up. You need to tout that you're new and exciting yet prove that you're credible. Vigilantly collect endorsements, mentions, partnerships, customer quotes, and other signs that you're awesome and here to stay.

Also, you're usually changing how an industry works. For example, Alice.com is changing how people buy household goods. You need to explain to potential users why learning to do things differently with you is worth their time. You also have to guide users through trying out your product or service.

Finally, think about who will represent your company on social networks. You need a personality or persona. Zappos.com, for example, has CEO Tony Hsieh and trained customer care employees to represent the company on social networks. Similarly, Grasshopper.com's ambassador of buzz speaks for the company on social media sites.

WhiteHouse.gov: From Archive to Media Property (in Three Years Flat)

On January 20, 2009, 1600 Pennsylvania Avenue wasn't the only address to change residents. The Bush administration also turned over the keys to WhiteHouse.gov when President Obama arrived. Surprisingly, the change mirrors the journey many of us face with our websites.

ARCHIVING RECORDS

During President Bush's two terms, WhiteHouse.gov was an archive of the president's communications and White House history. From 2005 to 2007, David Almacy oversaw WhiteHouse.gov as one of many responsibilities in his role as White House Internet and E-Communications Director. Almacy, currently a Senior Vice President of Digital Public Affairs at Edelman, talked with me about his approach.

"From a communication perspective, I viewed the website as the president's website and a literal archive of his events, speeches, written statements, and other executive communications. Though many in the federal government often wanted their content published on WhiteHouse.gov, we typically didn't post it unless it involved the president directly," explains Almacy.

The approach also synchronized communication from several areas within the White House. Almacy notes, "I kept in lockstep with the White House Press Office. For instance, if President Bush gave a speech, we provided the full transcript as well as photos, audio, video, and related policy links on the website."

Because that content was available *only* on the website, Almacy often evaluated the website's performance based on page view metrics.

REORGANIZING TO EMPHASIZE AND SHARE NEW RECORDS

In March 2007, Almacy released the biggest redesign of WhiteHouse.gov to date. The new design used the same platform but made the latest content easier to find. When it launched, Almacy described his approach this way:

"In addition to freshening the look and the feel of the site, our goal was to improve access to information about the president's speeches, events, and policies. Upgrades were made to streamline the code and better highlight existing features such as RSS news feed subscriptions, weekly email updates, audio podcasts, photos, and on-demand video."[1]

The redesign also made it easier for media websites to link to or reuse the content.

sidebar continues on next page

WhiteHouse.gov: From Archive to Media Property (in Three Years Flat) *continued*

CHANGING WITH TECHNOLOGY

In 2005, the Internet seemed to be maturing at lightning speed as sites like Facebook, Twitter, and YouTube were growing in popularity. "Changes in technology and social media happened very quickly. We embraced new digital channels when appropriate and in accordance with government policies," says Almacy.

For example, in 2007 Almacy produced the latest installment of Barney Cam, the popular annual holiday video featuring the First Dog (President Bush's Scottish Terrier, Barney), on WhiteHouse.gov and on iTunes, which pulled the file from WhiteHouse.gov servers. Other people published their own versions of Barney Cam on news sites, YouTube, and on their blogs. Though surprising at first, "We began to realize that we were quickly losing control of where our content was hosted, but that was OK," Almacy notes.

He also realized that the metrics for website success were changing. Almacy explains, "We had to consider more than specific page views on our website and look at exposure across these different digital channels." (For more about content evaluation, see Chapter 8.) Meanwhile, the incoming Obama administration had used social media on the campaign trail and expected to use it while governing. (For more about BarackObama.org, see Chapter 5.) That need led Robert Klause—then Web Manager and now Senior Practice Manager at Siteworx—to make a big change. He migrated WhiteHouse.gov to a new open-source platform (backend), Drupal.

"Based on how the Obama campaign website was run, I saw that the incoming administration had new requirements. The website would need to accommodate core archival content as well as more social elements and flexibility. That led me to consider options for a new platform. Ultimately, Drupal was the best choice to meet the requirements," says Klause.

PRODUCING AND DEBATING TODAY'S WHITEHOUSE.GOV

On January 20, 2009, a server switch launched the current WhiteHouse.gov at precisely 12:01 a.m. Director of New Media Macon Phillips has described it as "the place for the president and his administration to connect with the rest of the nation and the world."[2]

The site includes multiple blogs by many authors, photo galleries, podcast feeds, and integration with social networks. The content covers a variety of issues and stories, not only ones involving the president. It has the complexity and feel of a well-executed media property, with constant updates to content. WhiteHouse.gov has earned much praise and, at the same time, sparked an unprecedented debate.

On one hand, people who applaud the social aspects don't think it's social enough. For example, the blogs do not accept comments due to security concerns and problems with trollers (people who post inflammatory comments). Social media advocates want more two-way communication.[3]

sidebar continues on next page

WhiteHouse.gov: From Archive to Media Property (in Three Years Flat) *continued*

On the other hand, people who view the site increasingly as a media property see the traditionally clear lines between the government and the press blurring.

Phillips has said, "Historically the media have been able to draw out a lot of information and characterize it for people. And there's a growing appetite from people to do it themselves."[4]

However, if the only source of that information is WhiteHouse.gov, the White House alone is framing the content for people to characterize. (See an explanation of framing in Chapter 5.) For example, WhiteHouse.gov provides only highlights of most of the president's communications and no longer publishes most of the full transcripts, audio, and video. That concerns some people.

"They're beginning to create their own journalism, their own description of events of the day, but it's not an independent voice making that description," says Bill Kovach, journalist and founding chairman of the Committee of Concerned Journalists.[5]

Such debate seems healthy as WhiteHouse.gov pioneers new territory.

It's not hard to imagine that sustaining the current WhiteHouse.gov is a huge amount of work. Phillips plans strategy while being "beholden to the day-to-day communications operations of the White House," and he says "balancing those activities… is one of the biggest challenges."[6]

Keep watching WhiteHouse.gov closely. Its rapid rite of passage from communication archive to media outlet offers lessons for anyone with a website.

Small Business or Nonprofit

No matter what that friend-of-a-friend developer says, you don't need a lot of fancy technology to make a fantastic impression on the web. You *do* need solid content and design. A simple website based on a blog platform (such as WordPress) with a clean design and quality content will work well.

Like a startup, focus on showing your credibility. Also, make sure your content consistently explains the value of your product or service and advises people about relevant topics. For inspiration, think about questions you answer regularly and the answers that resonate best with your customers.

If you need help, it's available. I'm happy to see quality web professionals specialize in small business. One example is http://Zerogravitydesign.com, an agency that offers sensible design and content packages for small businesses and nonprofits.

STARTING WITH AN INTRANET LANDFILL

For employees of large companies, intranets could be an influential guide at work. But, intranets are often more of a hindrance than a help to employees trying to make decisions on the job. Large companies unknowingly treat the intranet as a dump, littering it with many intranet sites and applications from many different teams and departments. This situation is often viewed as a usability problem, but it's much more than that. It's a business process, content, and technology problem. Before an intranet landfill can truly help employees make decisions, you (or your team) must overhaul it.

Clean Up the Content

If your employer or client has an intranet content dump, here are a few quick tips to start cleaning it up:

1. Collect some evidence that the intranet needs help. (See Chapter 8 for evaluation approaches.)

2. For the short term, get rid of obviously old or low-quality content.

3. For the long term, I recommend
   - Better planning of published content
   - Structuring content to support business processes
   - Governing the archival, reuse, or removal of old content

4. Collect some evidence to show whether cleaning up the content helped.

To make the most of your content overhaul, consider how well your technology works with your content.

Mashup the Websites and Applications

For many companies, the intranet landscape looks like **Figure 7.1**, with websites and applications strewn here, there, and everywhere.

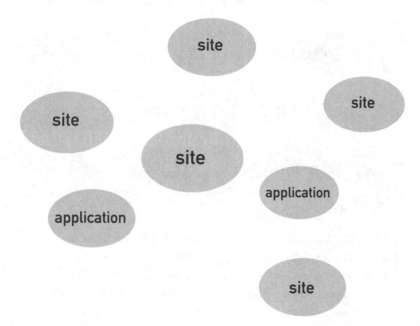

Figure 7.1: A scattered intranet landscape.

The content and data buried within these sites and applications are like needles in a gigantic haystack. A user has to remember which site or application does what and sort through lots of hay before finding a needle. What would be better? Melding those scattered sites and applications into a unified experience. Imagine that a user didn't have to rummage through each of those sites and applications but, instead, could simply go to her own intranet page and access the right content and data at the right time.

Turn Imagination into Reality with Interoperability

I used to think changing this intranet landscape for large companies was a fantasy. But, now, I have hope that it can become reality thanks to *interoperability*, the movement to make intranet websites and applications "talk" to each other. Interoperability is not a magic pill, it's an industry-wide collaboration. For example, Microsoft, IBM, Drupal, Alfresco, and other major vendors have agreed on and developed a protocol called Content Management Interoperability Services (CMIS). That protocol allows SharePoint, Drupal, and other products commonly used for intranet websites to communicate. CMIS plus some technological savvy can align scattered intranet sites (**Figure 7.2**).

Figure 7.2: A unified intranet landscape.

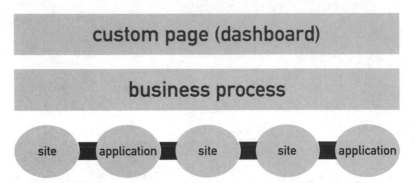

Make Intranet Technology Support, Not Drive, Your Business Process

Interoperability requires help from your information technology (IT) or development team. But, interoperability isn't an IT project. You (the business) must define the business processes, rules, and requirements that determine what content and data users see on their dashboards, and when. For example, you can align the dashboard that a marketing manager sees with your company's marketing cycle.

Why is your involvement so important? If you don't adapt technology to support your business process, your business process will adapt to your technology. I'm still shocked when I see a Fortune 500 company let a poorly planned intranet dictate how the company communicates with employees and how employees conduct day-to-day business. Claim—or reclaim—how you communicate and do business by defining what your intranet should do for employees.

Don't Be Your Intranet's Worst Enemy

If big businesses want their intranets to have a chance at being influential, they need to stop doing these things:

1. **Playing hot potato.** The intranet isn't a hot vegetable of any sort. Stop passing it from owner to owner. An intranet is a huge effort that requires a dedicated team or set of teams. Each time the intranet is passed to a different owner, you lose time, effort, and even morale.

2. **Denying the intranet an A team (or A team rewards).** Making the most of an intranet requires smart people from business and technology behind it. When you put the wrong people on the intranet team or fail to reward a good team, you risk making your intranet fail. Make the intranet a priority and value the people who make it work.

3. **Putting a bandage on a gaping wound.** When you add a social feature to your broken intranet, you're providing some temporary relief, not real healing. Fix the source of your intranet problems.

ROADBLOCKS WHILE RAISING AWARENESS

When you're trying to attract the right users through social networking, advertising, and search, you might run into obstacles, such as

- The great content divide
- Keyword crisis

THE GREAT CONTENT DIVIDE

If uncoordinated teams publish your social and advertising content, and that content links to your website content (which is likely published by still another team), you risk a rift in your brand's message or voice (**Figure 7.3**). A little variation is interesting, but inconsistency or contradiction damages your brand's credibility and confuses users about what you stand for. If the rift is big enough, you'll give users a shaky introduction to your website, not to mention your brand. No one likes a bait and switch.

Figure 7.3: Are your social, website, and advertising content miles apart?

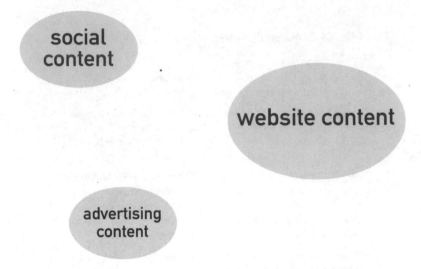

To cross the great content divide, put your editorial style guide and editorial calendar to work. And collaborate with all the teams who contribute content through regular meetings. As content strategist Sally Bagshaw explains,

"Show how web content fits in with the overall communication material of the organization. If the web team sits within a dedicated web or IT area, ensure there is some sort of liaison or relationship built with the marketing area so that key messages are reflected across all communication activities."[7]

KEYWORD CRISIS

To be found in search engines, your content probably includes keywords, or search terms that people use when looking for your topic, product, or service. For example, an innovation consultancy would want to be found if a user searched for "innovation." What if that content isn't getting the results you wanted for your keywords?

Make Sure It's Really a Crisis

Before you rip apart your content, make sure you actually have a crisis on your hands. For example, many people fret over bounce rates, a metric that indicates a user looked at your web page and then left without visiting other pages or following your call to action. When you're trying to raise awareness, bounces aren't necessarily bad as long as users remember you and return later. Usually, it's not realistic to think a user will discover you and then immediately buy your product or take the action you want them to take. (For more about evaluating content, see Chapter 8.)

If you think you have a real keyword crisis, then consider editing your content. *Audience, Relevance, and Search* by James Mathewson, Frank Donatone, and Cynthia Fishel offers some tips. Also consider using long tail keywords.

Remember Long Tail (Specific) Keywords

If your content, product, or service focuses on a topic with a lot of keyword competition, such as "innovation," consider using more specific keywords and phrases. Besides getting around the competition, specific keywords or phrases better match your content to how your users decide. For example, a user who is starting to think about innovation might search for "what is business innovation," while a user who is ready to do something about innovation in her job might search for "tips for innovative business culture." If a user becomes aware of you on the first search ("what is business innovation") and finds you later when he is ready to act ("tips for innovative business culture"), your chances of influencing action are very good.

ROADBLOCKS WHILE BECOMING LIKED AND TRUSTED

In this phase, you could face roadblocks that result from the challenges of managing day-to-day content needs while staying strategic.

MICROSITE MUSHROOMING

Large companies sprout microsites like mushrooms after a rain shower. These microsites usually support a promotion or campaign and become outdated quickly. Search engines will find old microsites, which risks confusing users and presenting an outdated version of the company's brand. A short-term fix, of course, is to take down old microsites. But to solve this problem for good, let's look at why it happens.

Many large companies have rather long development and production schedules. People in those large companies turn to microsites either as a way to avoid those schedules or in a panic after realizing they missed those schedules. Microsite sprawl is a sign that the website (and the production processes that support it) don't accommodate timely content well. Timely content is a legitimate need that deserves a well-thought-out solution. For example, you might consider using social networks or a well-planned blog instead of microsites. Or, you might develop some functionality to generate search-friendly landing pages. At the same time, marketing usually needs to plan content better. Even with improvements in the site, eleventh-hour demands for microsites need to stop. Think about the content life cycle and start an editorial calendar that includes campaigns and promotions.

STUCK IN A RUT

In this book, I've talked a lot about planning, consistency, and structure. Sometimes, that's misunderstood as "be boring and robotic." No one likes boring, and it's hard for users to identify with robots. The irony is that the better you plan, the more consistent your content quality, and the better organized your content, the *better your ability to shake things up every now and then*. If you handle your day-to-day content efforts smoothly, you can devote time and energy to something special. If you have a well-known message, voice, or approach, doing something different will stand out much more than if your content is typically haphazard.

Planning a Wow Moment

The greater irony is that you have to *plan* to do something special. The user experience consultancy Adaptive Path has called this creating "customer wow moments."[8] One example is Mint.com's new Goals feature, which combines the user's personal data and content with goals that the user sets to easily track financial goals ranging from vacation to retirement (**Figure 7.4**).

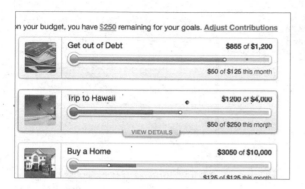

Figure 7.4:
Mint.com wows
customers with an
easy way to track
goals.

You can create special moments efficiently by repackaging existing content and data in a unique way. For example, the travel service Dopplr.com delighted its customers with a customized report of their travel activity, which was a clever repackaging of data and content dopplr.com already had. Some experts even suggest that such moments engender as much loyalty as discounts, points, or other typical marketing incentives.[9]

The editorial calendar and ongoing strategic evaluation of your content will help you avoid a rut.

ROADBLOCKS WHILE INSPIRING, MOTIVATING, AND HELPING ACTION

In this phase, you want users to act. You might face challenges with balancing motivation and instruction, providing proper support, and reassuring users of their actions.

MOTIVATING WHEN YOU SHOULD INSTRUCT—AND VICE VERSA

Asking users to act requires the art and science of influence in concentrate. If you don't get the balance right, you risk ruining your opportune moment with users. Persuasion expert BJ Fogg has found that for people to respond to a call (which he calls a "target behavior"), they must be motivated and able to act[10] (**Figure 7.5**).

Figure 7.5: BJ Fogg's Behavior Model shows that users must be motivated and able to act.

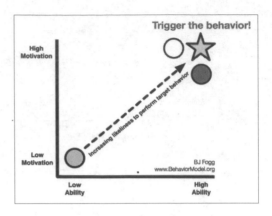

If you try to inspire users when they're already motivated, you'll slow them down and deter them from acting. If you focus on instructing users to act when they're not motivated, you'll come across as pushy and, likewise, deter them from acting. The better you understand the mix of motivation and instruction your users need, the better you can offer the right content to nudge them into action.

Behavior Wizard: A Planning Tool for Influencing Action

The Behavior Wizard is a research-based planning tool built by the Persuasive Technology Lab at Stanford University. The tool consolidates a wealth of insight and makes applying it easier than ever.

The Behavior Wizard asks questions about the behavior you want to change in yourself or others and a few questions about you. The result? A detailed guide to influencing the action delivered to your inbox.

Try the tool yourself at behaviorwizard.org.

SUPPORTING OFFLINE ACTION

Often, the action we want people to take—voting or getting travel vaccinations, for example—is not on the web. Help people get from your website to the action through very clear instructions. Also, try to make the instructions portable by print, email, or mobile access. Consider reminding people of the action, too.

For example, in rethinking the Travelers' Health website of the Centers for Disease Control and Prevention (mentioned in Chapters 4 and 5), we made finding a travel clinic—the place users go to get their shots—easier. For the short term, we also made printing the recommended vaccinations clear so patients can bring them to the clinic or doctor's office. For the long term, we started planning for mobile as a way for travelers to bring recommended vaccinations into the office or to get travel health tips on the go.

BUYER'S REMORSE

It's not a myth. People feel regret immediately after they buy something expensive (such as a car or a house) or make a big commitment. Counteract it by offering content that reassures people that they made a good investment of money or time. For example, link to such content in a confirmation or welcome email. Also, remind them that other people who made the same choice are satisfied, if not delighted. If possible, offer a way to connect with those people. Part of the power of the Obama campaign website was getting like-minded people together, as noted in Chapter 5.

SUMMARY

As you climb to clout, you'll likely hit roadblocks, but don't let them stop you. Understand them and overcome them. To track your progress, learn more about evaluating content in Chapter 8.

REFERENCES

1 David Almacy, Ask the White House at http://georgewbush-whitehouse.archives.gov/ask/20070301.html

2 Macon Phillips, Change Has Come to Whitehouse.gov at http://www.whitehouse.gov/blog/change_has_come_to_whitehouse-gov/

3 Clive Thompson, Clive Thompson on The Taming of Comment Trolls at http://www.wired.com/techbiz/people/magazine/17-04/st_thompson

4 The Washington Post, Macon Phillips on WhoRunsGov.com at http://www.whorunsgov.com/Profiles/Macon_Phillips

5 Jim Rutenberg, Adam Nagourney, "Melding Obama's Web to a YouTube Presidency" at http://www.nytimes.com/2009/01/26/us/politics/26grassroots.html

6   The *Washington Post*, Macon Phillips on WhoRunsGov.com at http://www.whorunsgov. com/Profiles/Macon_Phillips

7   Sally Bagshaw, Producing quality content with multiple contributors at http://johnnyhol- land.org/2010/10/12/producing-quality-content-with-multiple-contributors/

8   Colleen Jones, Using content to grow customer relationships at http://www.uxmatters. com/mt/archives/2009/06/using-content-to-grow-customer-relationships.php

9   Brandon Schauer, The long wow at http://www.adaptivepath.com/ideas/essays/ archives/000858.php

10 BJ Fogg, BJ Fogg's Behavior Model at http://behaviormodel.org/

8 PREPARE TO EVALUATE

· ·

You're following your plan. How do you know whether you're making progress? Evaluate whether your content is getting results, while keeping the right perspective on data. Let data inform, not distract from, your content decisions.

DO NOT MISTAKE DATA FOR SOLUTIONS, IDEAS, INSIGHTS, OR STRATEGIES.

—Gerald Zaltman and Lindsay Zaltman, consumer researchers

Today, a hiker can assess her progress on a climb using all kinds of data. She can learn her direction, elevation, distance traveled, the temperature, changes in barometric pressure, and much more from small but sophisticated gadgets. The question is not *whether* the hiker has data available but *which* data is most useful to her *when* she's on her journey. For example, elevation is helpful toward the middle and end of the journey, when the trail slopes sharply.

You face a similar situation. The question is not *whether* data about web content is available. Web analytic tools bring you lots and lots of data, from search analytics to keyword analysis to page views to conversion rates. And, you might even have offline data available, such as reasons people call your company. Unquestionably, lots of data is available.

The question is *which* data should you use *when*? Before we dive into the details of data, I invite you to consider a philosophy of evaluation. It's a philosophy rooted in an important question.

SHOULD DATA *INFORM* OR *DRIVE* YOUR CONTENT DECISIONS?

Data is most useful when it informs, not drives, content decisions. Investor Warren Buffett once joked, "A public-opinion poll is no substitute for thought." I sometimes quip a variation to clients—data[1] is no substitute for thought. I often see large organizations collecting enormous amounts of data and, in comparison, spending little effort thinking through what the data means and what to *do* about it. We're fortunate that modern technology makes getting the data relatively easy. But, *using* it well is hard.

What keeps people from using web data well? I believe it's two related, subtle myths:

- Data should decide for you.
- More data is better.

So, let's blast those myths.

DATA CAN'T AND SHOULDN'T DECIDE FOR YOU

At the end of the day (or a project), people—not data—are responsible for decisions about websites and their content. That's easy to forget. As user experience expert Jesse James Garrett has said, "Technology products are made by people and…someone, somewhere should get the credit when technology works well for us—or get the blame when it doesn't."[1]

You Can't Hide Behind Data

At times, I see people use data as an odd shield from responsibility. It's as if they want to look at the data for a few minutes, like shaking up a Magic 8 Ball, and watch the data's mystical answer appear. If the data can't answer, well, it's not their fault if they make the wrong decision. At the other extreme, some people get stuck in analysis paralysis. They gather more and more data as they delay decisions longer and longer, hoping for the data to answer so they don't have to. It's as if people want data to absolve them of thinking and making tough calls. (Truth be told, I'd find that wonderfully convenient on some hectic days.)

However, data doesn't work that way. Sometimes, you have to piece together data from several sources to see a complete picture. Sometimes, data makes you stop and think pretty hard—especially when what you see is not what you expected or wanted. And, sometimes, data can't save you from a tough decision. Most decisions require considering benefits, drawbacks, and tradeoffs. Data can't do that for you.

Faster Tools Don't Mean Faster Decisions

Web professionals are busy. Often, data tools are promoted as shortcuts to help them decide quickly. While gathering the data certainly gets faster, people's brains can't follow suit. No matter how much data or how many tools are available, people still need time to consider the data carefully. And in a crisis, you don't always have the luxury of time. Using data well during normal times can help you respond to a crisis more appropriately.

If the brain can process only so much data so quickly, that makes selecting the right data to monitor pretty important—enter the next myth to blast.

MORE ISN'T ALWAYS BETTER

Sometimes, you can have too much of a good thing. When people overload their minds with irrelevant data, they make decisions harder, not easier—and even less accurate.

Here's an example from the health industry. Magnetic resonance imaging (MRI) is a technology that allows doctors to see inside the body in amazing detail. It has helped clinicians understand the body better. MRI should make diagnosing tough problems such as back pain easier, right? I would have thought so. Turns out the MRI has led to so many wrong diagnoses and ineffective treatments for back pain that the American College of Physicians and the American Pain Society recommend *not* using the MRI for diagnosing back pain. As Jonah Lehrer, author of *How We Decide*, explains:

"Sometimes, more information and analysis can actually constrict thinking, making people understand less about what's really going on. Instead of focusing on the most pertinent variable ... doctors got sidetracked by the irrelevant MRI pictures."[2]

I believe the same thing happens with data for websites. Well-meaning people get distracted by the myriad of numbers they can collect—like the detail offered by an MRI—instead of paying attention to the important variables and thinking about their meaning.

I asked Jeff Chasin, an independent web analytics consultant, for his perspective. He notes:

"The dashboard of your car has *just enough* information to help you get where you're going without distraction or confusion. You can see and understand the amount of gas you have left or your current speed with a quick look. The presentation of your website data is usually the *opposite*: too much of a good thing. You need to know which data will help you achieve your goals and execute your tactics."

Before we take a look at that data, let's sum up the role of data in evaluating your content.

DATA IS YOUR EYES, NOT YOUR BRAIN

The point of data is to help you see your situation as it is. That's very valuable in the interactive world, where your website involves lots of stuff you can't see easily. (Unlike most hikers, you don't have an obviously marked trail.) Once you can see the situation clearly, then you can decide whether it's the way you want the situation *to be*. If not, you can make changes. If so, you keep on keeping on, and monitor your data. Over time, you might notice patterns and gain insights that inspire new ideas and find problems that need fixing. But, *you* make decisions—not data.

So, to help you stay in control of your data and your resulting content decisions, let's take a closer look at when and how to evaluate your efforts with which data.

WHAT AND WHEN SHOULD YOU EVALUATE?

Before you start looking at tools, metrics, or methodology, think about what you want to know at what point in your journey. Consider three main stages of developing influential web content:

- Before launch
- After launch
- Long after launch

For a brand new website, website section, social network presence, or major website redesign, you can evaluate content *before* you launch. The main goal is to explore and form the content direction to influence the results you want. You also need to evaluate content *after* launch to assess how well it influences. After your site has been around a while—or *long after* launch—you can assess how content is performing with an eye toward refining and deepening your influence.

BEFORE LAUNCH: FORMING DIRECTION

As you prepare to launch a new or redesigned website, evaluation can help you answer important questions at each major step:

- Refine strategy
- Develop concept or prototype
- Launch beta

Refine Strategy

At this point, gather data that helps you answer more specific questions about the context—your brand, users, forum, and timing. (For a discussion of understanding your context broadly, see Chapter 2.) Get a solid understanding of what your competitors are doing and saying. Focus on answering questions such as

- Which content topics and types do users want and need? Why?
- Which content topics and types do we already have?
- Which point of view and key messages fit the brand and users? Why?
- Which social networks do users frequent?
- Which pertinent keywords do users search?

Together, answers to these questions will help you see possible directions and assess which direction will most likely bring results.

If you have competitors, then also ask questions such as

- What content topics and types do competitors offer?
- What do users think of competitors' brands? Why?
- What point of view and key messages do competitors emphasize?
- What personas or personalities represent our competitors on social networks? How well do they engage with users?

If you're dealing with the redesign of an existing website, you can draw on insights from evaluating the existing website, too. (See Long After Launch: Deepening Influence.)

MORE INSIGHT

For a thorough explanation of the process to define a content strategy, see *Content Strategy for the Web*.

Develop Concept or Prototype

In this phase, you bring the strategy to life in a concept or prototype form so you can test how well it works. Your strategy becomes a rough draft of web content that you can show to users and then collect feedback. You have the chance to try a few options and revise before solidifying the direction. Consider answering questions about how well the content resonates, such as

- What style, tone, or voice resonates best with users?

- What persona/personality resonates best with users?

- What topics and conversations interest users?

- How do users respond to key messages?

Your answers will help you understand what works and what doesn't so you can make appropriate changes. For example, if the tone or voice of the content turns users off, you can adjust it.

At the same time, this phase is an excellent opportunity to find out whether web content is organized well and easy to use, whether its call to action is clear, and whether the action is easy to do. Think about questions such as

- Can users easily find and view or read the content?

- Do users understand and want to take the action?

- Can users complete the action?

Answering these questions will ensure that users can access your content and then act easily. For instance, if users have trouble noticing a call to action, you can change how it's worded or where it appears.

Launch Beta

New websites and website redesigns often go through a beta phase. During this stage, you have executed your direction and launched a version for users who are willing to try it. Your goals are to optimize the content, fix any problems, and get a preview of how users will respond before you unveil the website to the world. Consider questions such as

- Can you optimize critical screens or calls to action?

- Are there any problems, errors, or points of confusion to fix?

- What are users saying about the content?

The answers to such questions will help you refine important copy and address any last-minute problems. You can tweak the label on a critical button, for example. You also will gain insight into how users will respond to the actual launch, which will help you plan how to raise awareness of the website. For example, if your beta users say they love something about the content, such as the helpful product descriptions, emphasize that as a benefit when you announce the new website.

Table 8.1 summarizes key questions that will help you evaluate your website content before it launches. Now, let's turn to questions to consider after you launch.

USING KEY QUESTIONS

Every situation is different. Consider the questions for each stage as a guide. Not all of these questions will apply, and you might have some unique questions that you need to add. Adapt the questions as you see fit.

Table 8.1: Key Questions to Answer before Launch

PHASE	KEY QUESTIONS
Refine Strategy	Which content topics and types do users want and need? Why?
	Which content topics and types do we already have?
	Which point of view and key messages fit the brand and users? Why?
	Which social networks do users frequent?
	Which pertinent keywords do users search?
Develop Concept & Prototype	Which style, tone, or voice resonates best with users?
	Which persona/personality resonates best with users?
	Which topics and conversations interest users?
	How do users respond to key messages?
	Can users easily find and view or read the content?
	Do users understand and want to take the action?
	Can users complete the action?
Launch Beta	Can you optimize critical screens or calls to action?
	Are there any problems, errors, or points of confusion to fix?
	What are users saying about the content?

AFTER LAUNCH: GROWING INFLUENCE

After your new web presence is live, you can assess how well your content is helping you to raise awareness, become liked and trusted, and influence action. As you plan, it's useful to think about each phase consecutively. *In reality, you'll evaluate all phases simultaneously.* For example, you'll be raising awareness with new users while motivating action for users you've known for a while.

Raise Awareness

In this phase, find out whether your content is getting the attention of and attracting the right users. Focus on questions such as

- Do the right users know about you?
- Are users finding you and your content?
- Are users remembering you or returning to your content?

As you get answers, you can adjust your search engine optimization, social network efforts, or advertising. For example, if you find that your search engine advertising for some keywords does not bring the right users, consider advertising for different keywords or changing the ads.

Become Liked and Trusted

During this phase, gain insight into how your relationship with customers is developing. Consider questions along these lines:

- Do users identify with you?
- Do users think you're credible and trustworthy?
- Do users read and view your content?
- Are users sharing or talking about your content?
- Is the tone of your conversations with users appropriate?

The answers will give clues as to how users perceive and respond to you— and whether you need to make a change. As a simple example, if you find that few people share or comment on your content on Twitter (a social network), but many people do so on Facebook (a different social network), think about changing what you say on Twitter, creating content that's more appropriate to share on Twitter, or taking down your presence on Twitter altogether. Another example might be that users perceive you as snooty when you want to come across as smart; in this case, you can explore ways to adjust the tone of your content.

Motivate, Inspire, and Help Action

During this phase, you're interested in whether and how people are taking action. Consider questions such as

- Do users want to take action?
- Can users complete the action?
- Do users encourage others to take action?

As you discover the answers to these questions, you'll learn what prevents users from taking action and start overcoming those obstacles. For example, if users start to subscribe to your service but stop because they're not sure about your cancellation policy, you can clarify the policy.

Table 8.2 summarizes key questions to evaluate your website content after it launches. Before we explore ways to get answers, let's look at the questions to consider *long after* you launch.

Table 8.2: Key Questions to Answer After Launch

PHASE	EVALUATION QUESTION TO ANSWER
Raise Awareness	Do the right users know about you?
	Are users finding you and your content?
	Are users remembering you and returning to your content?
Become Liked and Trusted	Do users identify with you?
	Do users think you're credible and trustworthy?
	Do users read and view your content?
	Are users sharing or talking about your content?
	Is the tone of your conversations with users appropriate?
Motivate, Inspire, and Help Action	Do users want to take action?
	Do users complete the action?
	Do users encourage others to take action?

LONG AFTER LAUNCH: DEEPENING INFLUENCE

As you continue publishing web content, you need to understand how well your content sustains influence. You also can spot opportunities for content to deepen influence with your users. Evaluate long after launch to

- Maintain content.
- Identify usage patterns.
- Identify conversation patterns.
- Anticipate opportunities.

Maintain Content

Identify content that could confuse users or weaken your credibility. Think about questions such as

- Do we have any outdated or unused content?
- Do we have any broken links or recurring errors?
- Do we have any "dead" presence or accounts on social networking?

The answers to these questions will help you prune content that could undermine your influence and prevent users from taking action. For example, if you find a rogue microsite for an old campaign, take it down.

Identify Usage Patterns

Over time, check for patterns in how people discover and use your content. You can also learn more about who your users are. Ask questions along these lines:

- How do users find us and our content?
- When and how do users use our content?
- Do users return to us often?
- When and how do users take action?
- Are we attracting the users we expected?

Your inquiry is likely to reveal patterns that can help you plan future content, understand the loyalty of your users, and discover new users or audiences. For a real example, see the sidebar "Branded Traffic Is Better Traffic, Says Gawker Media."

Identify Conversation Patterns

If you connect with users on social networks or users talk with you in other ways (email, chat, or phone), then you can check for patterns in what users say. Think about questions such as

- What common questions do users ask us? When do they ask them?
- What are common themes in what users say?

As you discover answers to these questions, you'll find opportunities to better support your users' decisions with content. For example, if many users ask the same question after they sign up, consider whether and how to address the question sooner.

Tightening Up Internally

I recently talked with a thought leader in content strategy—Jeffrey MacIntyre of Predicate, LLC—about not only evaluating how your content performs over time but also examining your internal content processes.

"Content strategy is all about becoming a more effective publisher. Yet, one of the more overlooked applications for content strategy thinking is in fine-tuning internal processes like content production," notes MacIntyre.

Content is expensive—but you can optimize how you work with it, so long as you ensure your improvements address people, processes, *and* tools. Technology alone never works. As MacIntyre says, "finding ways to automate and introduce new efficiencies in existing workflows helps an organization get leaner and meaner, doing more with less. Given the pace at which so many web publishing tools improve these days, workflow redesign may be a welcome time and cost savings to an operation."

Of course, as you consider any change to your process, think about the full consequences.

"Be sure not to introduce new unforeseen complexities for others if you won't be implementing and 'living' the changes yourself," warns MacIntyre.

Anticipate Opportunities

Periodically, devote some time to thinking far ahead and to exploring opportunities. Ask questions such as

- Which emerging trends are likely to affect or help us? (For a start, see Chapter 11.)
- What are the content needs and interests of long term or repeat users?
- What are the content needs and interests of users we didn't expect to attract?

The answers to these questions will help you decide whether and how to respond to opportunities. For example, if your users love iPhone applications, consider whether any of your content is well suited to becoming an iPhone application.

Table 8.3 recaps key questions to evaluate your website content long after it launches. With a solid understanding of what to ask, you're ready to tackle getting answers.

Table 8.3: Key Questions to Answer Long After Launch

PHASE	EVALUATION QUESTION TO ANSWER
Maintain	Do we have any outdated or unused content?
	Do we have any broken links or recurring errors?
	Do we have any "dead" presence on social networking?
Identify Usage Patterns	How do users find us and our content?
	How do different types of users use our content?
	Do users return to us often?
	When and how do users take action?
	Are we attracting the users we expected?
Identify Conversation Patterns	What are common questions users ask us?
	What are common themes in what users say?
Anticipate Opportunities	Which emerging trends are likely to affect or help us?
	What are the needs and interests of long term or repeat users?
	What are the needs and interests of users we didn't expect to attract?

SUMMARY

To assess your progress toward clout, evaluate whether your web content is getting results. Get help with your evaluation from data. To make the most of data, first carefully consider the questions you want to answer. Once you have a firm grasp on the right questions, you can select the right evaluation methods to answer them. Learn more about how to evaluate in Chapter 9.

REFERENCES

1 Jesse James Garrett, *The Elements of User Experience* (Peachpit Press, 2002)

2 Jonah Lehrer, *How We Decide* (Houghton Mifflin Co, 2009)

9 EVALUATE WITH THE RIGHT METHODS

You're prepared to evaluate your content with the right questions. How do you get answers? Select the right mix of qualitative and quantitative methods.

ANY MEASUREMENT MUST TAKE INTO ACCOUNT THE POSITION OF THE OBSERVER.

—Jeanette Winterson, journalist

After you decide on the right questions to ask, pick the right methods of getting answers. Choose a combination of these two types of methods:

- Qualitative methods, which examine characteristics, or *qualities*.
- Quantitative methods, which count precise amounts, or *quantities*.

These methods work together, like art and science, to tell a complete story about your content. Quantitative methods help you understand *what* exactly is happening with your content, while qualitative methods give you rich insight into *why* it's happening. Neither type of method is superior to the other. You need both types.

Before launch, rely on qualitative methods to form a strategic direction. Use quantitative methods to verify and possibly refine the direction. After launch, monitor your website and its content with quantitative methods, then turn to qualitative methods when you need to deepen your understanding about a problem or opportunity (**Figure 9.1**).

Figure 9.1: You need both qualitative and quantitative methods.

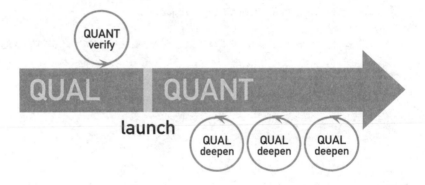

QUALITATIVE METHODS: UNDERSTANDING CONTEXT

Qualitative evaluation is extremely useful for three common scenarios:

1. You want to understand context better so you can decide on a strategic direction (before launch).

2. You want to understand why a problem is happening so you can decide on a solution (after launch).

3. You want to understand why an opportunity or unexpected result, such as attracting new users, is happening so you can decide how to respond (after launch).

Many content strategists and web writers take to qualitative research like fish to water. Why? This research is really about understanding context, and context is on the minds of many content strategists and writers.

There are many qualitative methods. For influential content, I find the most useful ones come down to talking to users and reviewing documents or content. As you might guess, these methods take time and collect a lot of data that isn't necessarily numerical. So, for each method, I offer a brief explanation and tips to use the method efficiently.

CONTENT AUDIT

What It Is

A detailed review of your content

When to Use It

Before launch or when you're making a big change to answer questions such as

- What content topics and types do we already have?
- What is the quality of the content?

Top Tips

- For refining strategy, get a good feel for the content by reviewing a sample of the most *common* and most *important* content.
- Review competitor content to understand competitors' ownership of content topics, point of view, and tone. You generally don't want to duplicate what your competitors are doing.

Good Resource

- *Content Strategy for the Web* by Kristina Halvorson (New Riders Press)

CONVERSATION REVIEW

What It Is

A qualitative review of conversations happening

- On social networks
- In user-generated content (e.g., blog comments or product reviews)
- In contact content (e.g., users' emails, chats, and calls to your company)

When to Use It

- Before launch to understand how users talk about your brand, topics, and competitors

- During beta to understand how users are responding to your content

- After launch to understand sources of confusion and to monitor tone, as well as who is contributing to the conversation

Top Tips

- Don't get lost in the weeds. Remember the point is to understand tone, themes, common words, and sources of confusion or problems.

- This review complements quantitative contact analytics and social analytics.

Good Resources

- *Engage* by Brian Solis (Wiley)

- *Observing the User Experience* by Mike Kuniavsky (Morgan Kaufmann)

TREND REVIEW

What It Is

A review of commentary, analysis, and outside research to identify business, technology, industry, content, and other trends

When to Use It

- After launch to understand areas of change and opportunity

Top Tips

- Devote time to monitoring trends, especially over the next several years when lots of changes will happen. If you don't, you'll fall behind fast.

Good Resources

These are a few of my favorite resources, which lean toward business and content strategy:

- Brain Traffic Blog (including other blogs and resources listed there)— http://blog.braintraffic.com

- CMS Wire—http://www.cmswire.com

- Econsultancy.com—http://econsultancy.com

- Edelman—http://www.edelman.com

- Forrester—http://www.forrester.com

- Gartner—http://www.gartner.com

- Harvard Business Review—http://hbr.org

- McKinsey and Company—http://www.mckinsey.com

- The Nielsen Company—http://www.nielsen.com

- PaidContent.org—http://paidcontent.org

- Pew Internet and American Life—http://www.pewinternet.org

- Scatter/Gather (Razorfish blog)—http://scattergather.razorfish.com/

USER INTERVIEW

What It Is

An in-depth, structured conversation with a user, usually conducted in person

When to Use It

- Before launch to understand users better and get their feedback on content messages, concepts, or prototypes

- After launch to understand the cause of a problem or an unexpected result

Types

- Interview only

- Interview and activity that asks users to try out your content

Top Tips

- Talk to people who *truly* represent your users or the people you want to attract. It's the only way to get the right perspective.

- Interview at least five people for each user type or persona you want to reach. It's the best way to see patterns in what users say and do.

- Don't spend so much time with the user on *finding* content that you have no time to discuss the content itself.

- For interviews about content concepts or prototypes, provide more than one option when possible. People provide richer feedback when they can compare and contrast options.

- After you write your interview questions and before you interview the first user, do a dry run with a colleague. Work out kinks and correct any unclear or leading questions.

- This method complements most quantitative methods.

Good Resources

- *Observing the User Experience* by Mike Kuniavsky (Morgan Kaufmann)
- *Card Sorting* by Donna Spencer (Rosenfeld Media)
- "10 Tips for Testing a Content Concept" by Content Science— http://content-science.com/expertise/reports-tools/

QUANTITATIVE METHODS: MEASURING WHAT'S HAPPENING

By now, you probably sense that I have a healthy skepticism of quantitative methods. It's not because I hate numbers. It's because I see quantitative methods abused and manipulated to justify unwise content decisions. Surprisingly, I don't see this misuse from executives about return on investment (ROI). Every director, vice president, and C-level executive I've worked with understands the value of qualitative research coupled with quantitative measures. I see the manipulation of numbers more from overly zealous usability professionals and from misguided marketing managers. (I mean no offense to all the excellent usability and marketing professionals out there.) Quantitative numbers without qualitative context are, at worst, a misleading power trip and, at best, unclear.

If you like words, then quantitative numbers might seem like a daunting foreign language. Not to worry. Why? Well, for one thing, numbers are fallible. They have limitations. "I can poke a hole in any number we track," says one of my business intelligence friends. For another thing, numbers can and should be translated into a useful explanation. The key is to understand what the numbers are measuring and whether those measurements help you understand what's happening with your content.

There are many quantitative methods and gobs of quantitative tools. Below, I highlight the methods I find most useful for web content. For methods with lots of tools available, I list an example or sample tool(s). New tools become available all the time, however, so check out your options. For smaller businesses and nonprofits, I have flagged tools that offer a suitable price and features with an asterisk (*).

SURVEY

What It Is
A series of multiple choice, fill-in-the-blank, and open-ended questions about user demographics, preferences, expectations, and interests

When to Use It
- Before launch to verify important qualitative findings about users, such as what content topics interest them and how they perceive your brand or idea
- After launch to monitor content satisfaction, users' perceptions, and user demographics

Top Tips
- Word survey questions carefully so they are clear and aren't biased toward a particular answer.
- For a survey to count as a quantitative method, a lot of people (large sample size) need to complete the survey.
- Use open-ended questions sparingly. They offer a chance for users to explain an answer further but shouldn't be the core of your survey. Qualitative research is better to answer open-ended questions.
- An ongoing quarterly survey is highly useful. You can add and remove questions regarding specific campaigns or timely content as needed.

Types and Tools
A variety of web-based tools are available:
- Custom survey using SurveyMonkey* (http://www.surveymonkey.com) or Survey.com*
- Syndicated survey using American Customer Satisfaction Index (includes content questions)
- Poll (mini survey) using Twitter* or LinkedIn*

Good Resource

- *Observing the User Experience* by Mike Kuniavsky (Morgan Kaufman)

REMOTE USER TEST

What It Is

A user interview and activity (see User Interview) conducted through a web-based tool, not in person

When to Use It

- Before launch to test how well a concept or prototype works for users

Top Tips

- Plan the protocol (series of tasks and questions) carefully so users can move through the test itself easily.

- For the test to count as a quantitative method, a lot of people (large sample size) need to complete the test.

- Do a dry run with a colleague. Work out kinks and correct any unclear or leading questions.

Types and Tools

- Self-guided test using Usertesting.com*
- Automated test using Keynote

Good Resource

- *Remote Research* by Nate Bolt and Tony Tulathimutte (Rosenfeld Media)

MULTIVARIATE AND A / B TEST

What It Is

A comparison of how different versions of important pages (such as product pages or landing pages) perform on your live website

When to Use It

- Before launch (during beta) to test different headings, buttons, arrangements of content, images, and similar variations on critical pages

- After launch to test small variations to critical pages or task flows

Top Tips

- The more variations you test, the longer it will take to get results.

- This method tells you which variation performs best with users but does not tell you why. Consequently, it's hard to compile lessons and principles that you can easily apply to other situations.

- For an example of A/B testing, see the sidebar Quality Content Books More Hotel Rooms for Holiday Inn in Chapter 2.

Tools

- Google Website Optimizer*

- Optimost

WEBSITE ANALYTICS

What It Is

Detailed statistics about how visitors use your website

When to Use It

- Before launch (during beta) to monitor performance

- After launch as your main source of quantitative data about users interacting with your web content

Top Tip

- Get help setting up and interpreting analytics from a business intelligence (BI) or web analytics professional—even if you're a smaller business. (See the sidebar The Value of Business Intelligence for Businesses Big and Small.)

Useful Measurements and Metrics

- Quantity/Scale
    - Page views
    - Unique visitors
- Quality/Depth
    - Time on site
    - Number of pages viewed
    - Bounce rate

- Return visitors
- Branded traffic (See the sidebar Branded Traffic Is Better Traffic, Says Gawker Media.)
- Action
  - Conversion rate
  - Bounce rate
  - Abandonment rate

Tools

- Google Analytics*
- Omniture
- SiteCatalyst

Good Resource

- *Web Analytics 2.0* by Avinash Kaushik (Sybex)

SOCIAL AND REPUTATION ANALYTICS

What It Is

Measurements of how users are talking about and referring to you on social networks

When to Use It

After launch to

- Monitor the tone of conversation.
- Identify and respond to problems or misunderstandings.
- Understand your influence over time.

Top Tips

- Give your effort time to realize growth and depth. Don't expect a viral sensation with every post or status. Longevity (sticking around a while), consistent content quality, and building a loyal community are more important to your results.
- The tools in this area are changing and evolving all the time. Focus on tools that offer useful data.

■ For responding to problems, this method complements contact analytics and the qualitative method of conversation review.

Types and Tools

■ Blog authority using Technorati* (indicates how many sites link to yours)

■ Blog subscribers using Feedburner*

■ Name/brand mentions using Google Alerts,* Reputation Defender,* or Radian6

■ Twitter using Klout* or Twitalyzer* (use the detailed metrics, not the single score)

■ Number of relevant followers on Twitter and friends on Facebook

Good Resources

■ *Web Analytics 2.0* by Avinash Kaushik (Sybex)

■ *Engage* by Brian Solis (Wiley)

SEARCH AND KEYWORD ANALYTICS

What It Is

Measurements of the words people use when they look for content through search engines such as Google and Bing (external search) and search on your website (internal search)

When to Use It

■ Before launch to understand how users look for the topics you plan to cover in your web content

■ After launch to understand how users enter your website and monitor changes in search terms

Top Tips

■ Users search on different types of words at different stages of their relationship with you. As a simple example, the better users know you, the more likely they are to use your specific brand or product name. (See the sidebar Branded Traffic Is Better Traffic, Says Gawker Media.)

■ Look for opportunity in long tail keywords, which tend to be more specific terms. Fewer competitors will be fighting your content for attention.

Branded Traffic Is Better Traffic, Says Gawker Media

Gawker Media has found that when users ask for their media websites by name, the users explore the sites more deeply and are more likely to come back. Gawker Media calls this discovery *branded traffic*.

"Branded traffic describes the segment of visitors who come to Gawker Media properties by typing in the URL of the site directly or by querying a search engine for the name of one of our titles. Those two major groups comprise a very valuable core audience for us—visitors who know us and ask for us by name," says Erin Pettigrew, Gawker Media's Marketing Director.

Clever. What inspired her to put those measurements together into a new metric that focuses on quality, not quantity?

"I was looking for a way to articulate the incredibly strong relationship that some of our readers have with our publishing brands and explain that to marketers. We've long known by intuition that some of our visitors come to us for our brand, while others come to us for specific pieces of content. For brand marketers looking to cultivate awareness through ad programs, that first segment is the Holy Grail," Pettigrew explains.

I am sold. What about marketers looking to advertise?

"We're definitely seeing some marketer interest as it has helped us quantify some of our more qualitative selling points. Another way to think of it is that the web has for so long differentiated media properties by their *scale*. But now that most of the consequential properties are in the range of tens of millions to hundreds of millions of visitors, those scale numbers are starting to become meaningless. The traditional reach metrics of unique visitors and page views are going nowhere fast."

But being a pioneer isn't without challenges. Even though the traditional reach metrics should probably die, the online advertising system keeps them alive.

"Page view isn't dead until we stop using it for display advertising," notes Alan Segal, Senior Manager of Business Intelligence and Platform Specialists for Cox Media Group. "It will take large media properties to set the wheels of change in motion."

Pettigrew remains hopeful that other large media properties will follow suit. She notes, "Branded traffic is still a bit of an unorthodox metric. Because we're the only ones who offer it, marketers can't use it yet to compare media properties. I'd be interested to see other publishers' versions of this type of metric."

Me, too. Considering that most marketers are now both advertisers *and* publishers, the lessons from this metric will run deep.

Tools

- KeywordDiscovery
- WordTracker
- Google AdWords Keyword Tool*
- Google Analytics*
- Omniture
- SiteCatalyst

Good Resources

- *Web Analytics 2.0* by Avinash Kaushik (Sybex)
- *Audience, Relevance, and Search* by James Mathewson, Frank Donatone, Cynthia Fishel (IBM Press)
- *Search Analytics* by Louis Rosenfeld and Marko Hurst (for your own website's search analytics; Rosenfeld Media)

CONTACT ANALYTICS

What It Is

Measurements of how and why users contact you (by email, call, chat, etc.) and how they respond to your contact (especially by email)

When to Use It

- After launch to identify and respond to problems, questions, or misunderstandings
- After launch to understand whether and how users respond to your email update or newsletter

Top Tips

- Look for opportunities to prevent problems or misunderstandings through better content.
- Look for trends or changes in the reasons why people contact you as their relationship with you evolves.

Tools

- Customer relationship management (CRM) tools such as SAP
- Call, email, and chat logs*
- Email marketing tools such as iContact* and MailChimp*

Good Resource

- *Observing the User Experience* by Mike Kuniavsky (Morgan Kaufman)

OFFLINE METRICS

Often, the action you want people to take is offline. You have to get creative about how to measure that action or signs that the action has happened.

For example, the Get Yourself Tested campaign mentioned in Chapter 2 (at www.itsyoursexlife.org) encourages teens to get tested for STDs. So, an important metric for success is whether teens get tested. That's exactly what the campaign sponsors—MTV and Kaiser Family Foundation— measured. In April 2009, for instance, they found that the number of teens who were tested for STDs in Planned Parenthood clinics doubled.[1]

SYNDICATED RESEARCH

What It Is

Research conducted by an independent company or organization and often sponsored by several companies within an industry

When to Use It

- After launch to identify and understand trends
- After launch to monitor competitive rankings in customer satisfaction

Top Tips

- Look at the research tools so you understand exactly what the research is measuring. For instance, if the research is the result of a survey, review the questions asked in the survey.

- Syndicated research often relies on panels of representative users. Find out whether those users represent your ideal users well and, consequently, apply to your situation.

Tools

These tools vary by industry, but a few common ones include

- ComScore
- Nielsen NetRatings
- J.D. Power and Associates

Good Resource

- *Web Analytics 2.0* by Avinash Kaushik (Sybex)

USING EVALUATION METHODS

Consider the list in Table 9.1 as a reference to help you plan, not a strict prescription. Use the methods that will best answer your most important evaluation questions.

Table 9.1: What Evaluation Methods to Try and When to Try Them

FOR THIS PHASE...	TRY QUALITATIVE METHODS...	WITH QUANTITATIVE METHODS...
Before	Content Audit	Search and Keyword Analytics
	Conversation Review	
	User Interview	Survey
		Remote User Test
		Multivariate and A/B Test
After and Long After	User Interview	Survey
		Website Analytics
	Conversation Review	Social and Reputation Analytics
		Search and Keyword Analytics
		Contact Analytics
		Offline Analytics
	Trend Review	Syndicated Research

The Value of Business Intelligence for Businesses Big and Small

A good relationship with a BI or web analytics professional can help you get value out of quantitative web data. I talked with two of my colleagues, Jeff Chasin (web analyst consultant) and Alan Segal (Senior Manager of Business Intelligence and Platform Specialists for Cox Media Group) about the benefits.

CORRECT IMPLEMENTATION OF ANALYTIC TOOLS

Many analytics tools are available. A BI professional or web analyst can help match your content questions with tool(s) that give the best answers and that work together well.

As Chasin notes, "Tools and technology don't matter nearly as much as an experienced web analyst who can help turn your goals and objectives into a measurable system."

A web analyst also implements analytic tools correctly so you can trust their measurements. For example, web analytic tools require that you include specific coding on your website.

SET UP OF INTEGRATED AND CUSTOMIZED DASHBOARDS

A BI professional knows how to combine different sources of quantitative data into a dashboard. For example, you might want to combine syndicated research with your website analytics and contact analytics. Beyond that, you can customize dashboards for different people's roles—very handy for large organizations.

For example, "A sports editor for one of our news websites wants to see only the data that relates to the sports content," Segal explains.

Creating such dashboards requires a lot of effort, however.

"Connecting various data systems and creating reports using high-end business intelligence tools is not a minor investment. Most enterprise-level organizations can get the ROI they need to connect these systems because of their large scale," says Chasin.

sidebar continues on next page

The Value of Business Intelligence for Businesses Big and Small *continued*

. . . .

HELP WITH INTERPRETATION

"Numbers in isolation are only that. They need context," says Segal. A BI professional can help interpret the numbers in a useful way. "The story of metrics is most compelling when it considers the user experience cycle and the business cycle," notes Segal.

For example, most of Cox Media Group's more than 100 television, radio, and web properties focus on *local markets*, such as a particular city or geographic region. That has led Segal to focus the metrics on understanding whether *local people* use the websites.

"If CNN.com highlights a story on one of our websites and drives lots of people from outside the market to the site, that's great. But, we're less interested in having lots of fly-by visitors and more interested in having people within those local markets use the sites frequently and deeply. To understand that, we have to unpack the numbers beyond page views and unique visitors. I also focus on insights that we can actually apply or act on."

OPTIONS FOR SMALLER BUSINESSES AND NONPROFITS

A smaller business or nonprofit doesn't need a team of BI professionals. Instead, a BI consultant can set up a useful system and then help maintain it.

"Hiring an experienced consultant for a few hours each month can provide your business with a valuable return on a relatively inexpensive investment," explains Chasin.

He adds, "Nonprofits can take advantage of programs like The Analysis Exchange, where experienced practitioners volunteer their time to improve the websites of nonprofit organizations."

SUMMARY

The right mix of qualitative and quantitative methods will help you get answers to your evaluation questions. As you discover answers, you need to decide whether you're on the right path to clout or need to change course. Learn more about adjusting in Chapter 10.

REFERENCES

1   Get Yourself Talking, Get Yourself Tested by Kaiser Family Foundation at http://www.kff.org/entpartnerships/mtv2/gyt.cfm

10 ADJUST

· ·

You're evaluating your progress toward clout with the right methods. How do you respond to what you find? You will likely need to adjust your content to address a problem, make the most of a success, or adapt to change. As you decide how to adjust, involve the right people and consider the right criteria.

WE CANNOT DIRECT THE WIND, BUT WE CAN ADJUST THE SAILS.

—Unknown

The purpose of evaluating your web content is to understand whether and how your content is getting results. When you understand that well, you can decide whether and how to make changes. Tracy V. Wilson, Site Director for HowStuffWorks.com, explains it this way:

"When we're looking at metrics, we're looking at them in light of how we already know our articles work, how we know they're structured, how we anticipate that an average reader would come in and go through the article from beginning to end. And we can do the same thing for different types of content. So, we have articles, we have top ten lists, top five lists, quizzes, image galleries...and we've developed a different sense of what 'normal' is for each of those.

"So, we're able to look at when something is deviating from our idea of normal and try to figure out why that deviation would take place. We also use metrics a lot in day-to-day planning, like planning what to feature on our home page...deciding whether that day's home page was successful; a lot of that is coming from numbers and whether people's behavior on the site that day is matching up with...what we're thinking of as the typical user behavior."[1]

WHEN SHOULD YOU CHANGE COURSE?

Most commonly, you'll want to make changes when you see something that isn't simply normal, such as

- Signs of problems
- Signs of success
- Signs of changing context

Let's look at each of these situations more closely.

SIGNS OF PROBLEMS

I've been brutally honest throughout this book, so why stop now? You'll see signs of problems, or at least unexpected results, more often than you'd like. For example, when I worked for Cingular Wireless (now AT&T), we found problems with the experience new customers had. Quantitative and qualitative data about why new customers called Cingular Wireless suggested that many questions could be prevented with better communication and content. Another example is the large retailer that came to me after its website redesign launch because its shopping cart abandonment rate had increased—the wrong direction! As Scott Thomas noted in Chapter 5, a website is like an "organism," and growing pains are the nature of the beast. To help you address them, consider these questions.

How Big Is the Problem?

Get a sense of the consequences so you can prioritize handling the problem. A big problem is an obstacle preventing you from getting results. A small problem is a bump in the road. Sometimes, a collection of small problems is the symptom of a big problem. For example, in the case of Cingular Wireless, support questions from new customers were a symptom of a bigger problem with how the company welcomed new customers.

Is Content the Only Source of the Problem?

To solve the problem, you need to understand the cause. Sometimes content is the cause, and sometimes content is partly the cause, along with design and technology. Cross-referencing your data and doing qualitative research will help you better understand the source so you can think of appropriate solutions. (For an example, see the sidebar Evaluation of a Health Website Reveals Problems—and Ideas for Solutions.)

How Can You Prevent the Problem in the Future?

Besides solving the problem now, what lesson can be learned so you don't recreate the problem later? Communicate the lesson learned to your team. Building this historical knowledge is an invaluable benefit of working on an in-house content team.

Evaluation of a Health Website Reveals Problems— and Ideas for Solutions

When the Centers for Disease Control and Prevention (CDC) thought about improving the Travelers' Health website, they started with their data. Travelers' Health is one of CDC's top five most-visited websites, with 9.5 million visits and 31 million page views in 2009 alone.

Those numbers are impressive, but Travelers' Health saw an opportunity to improve. Communication and Education Team Lead Kelly Holton examined data from CDC's call center. She noticed that the center received about 3,000 travel-related calls each month, and 70 percent of those were about travel vaccines. Qualitative (anecdotal) evidence suggested many people who called had *already* visited the Travelers' Health website, but it hadn't answered their questions.

Holton thought the website could better help those callers—and other users. She explains, "I was concerned about the number of people who were calling because they couldn't find travel vaccine information. I knew it was time to do something different to help drive our content strategy. I felt we needed to find out what users really think about and do with our content."

So, Holton led a project to test the website with real travelers. The qualitative results confirmed that a change was in order—and revealed more about *why*.

"We found that most people could not easily find the vaccination information. What's more, when we showed users the information, they became confused about what it meant and what they should do. Users couldn't easily get what they needed from the website and then take the right next step," notes Holton.

At the same time, I assessed the website and discovered opportunities to consolidate and clarify its content as well as to encourage action. (For details, see the presentation Testing Content: Early, Often, and Well by Colleen Jones and Kevin O'Connor at http://www.slideshare.net/leenjones/content-testing-early-often-well.)[2]

Emboldened with data, Holton gained support to take the Travelers' Health website in a new direction. The future holds a new focus on usable, influential content and more testing to confirm what works and what doesn't.

"We will test different concepts as we revamp the Travelers' Health website. And, as we implement changes, we'll keep track of our metrics to ensure the changes have positive impact," says Holton.

SIGNS OF SUCCESS

With time, you'll overcome problems and have success—the results you want. To make the most of it, consider these questions.

How Big Is the Success?

Get a sense of the scale so you can benchmark other successes against it and tell others about it. Are you breaking any records? Are you the first to achieve a result? Have you pioneered a new approach? Are you surprised by the success? For example, when I led a project to revamp the welcome experience for Cingular Wireless, we found that the new experience led the industry at the time. We executed a simple concept of welcoming a new customer through concise, useful, customized content very well. We took a rundown of the service plan and mobile device, an explanation of billing and the first bill, and tips to manage their account, then we packaged it as the Cingular Service Summary. Because no other wireless provider had anything like that at the time, the CSS earned attention in trade publications, kudos from customers, reduced call volume, and an executive award.

Another example is InterContinental Hotels Group's (IHG) pilot of quality photos and copy (explained in depth in Chapter 2), where the statistically significant increase in hotel bookings far exceeded expectations.

Why care about these things—for bragging rights? Not exactly. Understanding the scale will help you tell the story to your boss and to stakeholders so you get more support for your efforts. At Cingular Wireless, I gained support to revamp other aspects of the customer experience, such as improving the experience for customers who ordered service and devices through the website, rather than the retail store. IHG won approval to refresh the content for all Holiday Inn hotels.

Is Content the Only Source of the Success?

To make the success happen again, understand the complete cause. In the case of Cingular Wireless, the cause was a combination of technology, well-written and structured dynamic content, and information design. The effort was extremely complicated because of all the dynamic content—and consequently the business rules and requirements—behind it. To the customer, the summary was two pages of content. Behind the scenes, we actually had many different core templates of the summary depending on the customer and plan, plus English and Spanish variations.

In the case of IHG, the cause was clearly better quality content. In the case of North Carolina State University (see the sidebar Home Page Reclaims Homecoming at NC State University), the cause was editorial planning, quality content, design, and technology. People will want to know the secret of your success. The better you can explain it to your boss and stakeholders, the more likely it is that you'll get the budget and thumbs up to do it again.

How Can You Make It Happen Again?

What lessons can you learn from the success and apply to other areas? For example, Cingular Wireless applied the insights gained to other aspects of the customer experience. IHG is applying the lessons learned from Holiday Inn to other hotel brands. NC State University has taken its approach to homecoming and applied it to other occasions. Make the most of your success by figuring out how to use its lessons in other ways.

Home Page Reclaims Homecoming at NC State University

Homecoming. This single annual football game draws thousands of North Carolina State University alumni back to campus to reconnect with the school and support the Wolfpack. It also draws them to the university website.

THE OPPORTUNITY
Director of Web Communications Tim Jones and his team saw homecoming as an opportune moment and made the most of it through carefully planned home page content.

"Alums and their families use ncsu.edu as a directory service for the Alumni Association or Athletics sites, and we've got a chance to influence them with great content for the seconds they spend on the university home page," says Jones.

THE PLAN
To get ready, Jones's team reviewed the website's past treatments of homecoming.

"Historically, our approach to homecoming on the home page involved assembling existing event schedules and descriptions and crafting an intentionally vague home page teaser that fit into the space allowed by the CMS (content management system). The homecoming football game was just another event on the calendar," Jones explains.

The schedule was the story. Jones felt they needed a better approach.

sidebar continues on next page

Home Page Reclaims Homecoming at NC State University *continued*

Convinced that they could create content that would help reclaim homecoming as a week, not just a football game, Jones developed a weeklong run of content that would

- Evoke nostalgia and inspire pride in alumni.
- Present touchstones of the NC State brand.
- Engage students, faculty, and staff in a university tradition.

"The plan was to publish a new piece of the package every day leading up to the homecoming game, teasing the coming day's content with each new piece," notes Jones.

Jones's team worked with the known enthusiasm and passion for football, using athletics as bookends for the content plan. The week started with the history and tradition of the athletics facilities and programs. The guts of the week showcased homecoming-related activities and events that told the story of NC State's student leadership, the university's commitment to service, and the evolving NC State community. The week ended with a game day preview and a video interview with the alumnus who saved the homecoming parade from extinction.

Alumni and current students—two important audiences for homecoming content—come to the home page with some expectation of how the content looks. To show that the week was special, Jones felt they needed to present the homecoming content in a unique way. His team created a new home page template for their CMS.

"We blew up the home page for the week and filled the top of the page each day with a focused, bold image paired with strong type treatments and minimal home page copy. Read More links pushed to story pages. We populated those story pages with a mix of modern photography, art, videos, and a healthy number of historic images," Jones explains.

THE RESULTS

On its first day alone, the homecoming content earned twice as many page views as most of the website's feature stories earned in an entire week. By the end of the week, the homecoming package had nearly six times the clickthrough rate of an average week's feature content. Readers stuck around, too—the overall exit rate was less than half that of an average feature story.

The results exceeded everyone's expectations. This new approach quickly became part of the plan for the 2010 homecoming. The success led NC State to try similar editorial planning and to reuse the special home page template for other notable occasions.

Jones explains, "We constantly use this story as a case study to get more support than ever for our content efforts."

SIGNS OF CHANGING CONTEXT

Our websites and the Internet in which they live are like ecosystems. They evolve. As they evolve, context—users, brand, timing, forum, and desired result—often changes. Those changes can and should affect our web content.

Here are examples of some changes you might face:

- You attract different users than you expected. For example, in the early days of the Internet, CDC expected CDC.gov to attract public health and clinical professionals. They did, *and* they attracted a huge number of consumers.

- Your business or organization changes its goals, which changes the results you want and possibly your brand. IHG, for instance, decided to refresh the Holiday Inn brand online and offline.

- A new forum arrives on the scene. For example, Twitter and Facebook matured very quickly.

How Big Is the Change?

Is the change large, such as attracting many unexpected users, or small, such as attracting a small segment of users you didn't anticipate? Is it a small change that seems to be growing, such as the rapid rise of social media? Does it seem permanent or temporary? Is it consistent with industry or other trends? Cross-referencing your data will help you assess whether the change is a fluke or a growing trend and, consequently, whether you should invest time and resources to address it.

Is the Change an Opportunity or a Threat?

Think about the consequences of the change and how to respond. Is attracting unintended users an opportunity to reach a new audience or a new type of customer? Or is it taking time and resources away from reaching the users you intended?

50-Year-Old Health Care Brand Engages Users on Facebook Thanks to a Conversation Calendar

Creating a conversation calendar is an essential step to take before diving into the new forums offered by social media. The content development firm SPROUT Content shared their experience with using a conversation calendar to help an established health care brand succeed on Facebook.

"By planning your content on a conversation or editorial calendar, you create purposeful messaging that gives fans and followers a compelling reason to come back. From promotions and specials to topical and timely posts, a conversation calendar creates engaging content that connects with your audience and sparks a two-way conversation," explain SPROUT Content co-founders Dechay Watts and Debbie Williams.

THE OPPORTUNITY

A 50-year-old health care brand in the United States was starting to incorporate social media into their marketing efforts and had clear, actionable objectives. The goals were to

- Amplify current brand initiative content and generate excitement for major SKUs.

- Build equity by creating meaningful social connections.

- Drive loyalty by building relationships with more consumers, thereby creating brand advocates.

- Drive trial of new and existing products.

The brand had established a Facebook page but was not updating it regularly or posting comments that encouraged interaction.

THE PLAN

SPROUT Content developed a conversation calendar of three posts per week, written in the third person, with a fun and playful tone.

"Each message clearly dialed back to one of three specific content buckets (brand strategies) and end benefits to resonate with the target audience. We developed many posts as conversation starters, asking questions to stimulate audience engagement, likes, retweets, and sharing. Other posts focused on information that fans would find interesting and timely topics that corresponded with upcoming holidays and events," note Watts and Williams.

Each post positioned the brand as the leader and expert in its category, while keeping the user experience conversational.

sidebar continues on next page

50-Year-Old Health Care Brand Engages Users on Facebook Thanks to a Conversation Calendar *continued*

. . . .

THE RESULTS

The Facebook page launched a week prior to the conversation calendar initiative. It had only 14 fans. By the end of the first month, the brand had generated over 22,000 fans and consistent interaction.

As the fan base grew, people began to make comments such as "I use *brand name* everyday. Any coupons anywhere?" Because the brand knew what post would be coming up next, it could respond with places to find special offers, further enhancing brand loyalty, and teasers like "Check back later this week for more specials."

The brand could also track the type of interaction their target audience responded to. After one post that featured a quote from a famous person received 265 "likes" and 31 comments, more quotes from famous people about related topics were incorporated into the calendar.

This data guided future content decisions. As Watts and Williams explain, "We reviewed this type of data each month, and it guided the following month's conversation calendar, continually building on topics and subjects that the target audience found of interest."

HOW SHOULD A WEB CONTENT DECISION WORK?

If you need to adjust your content, then you'll need to decide how best to adjust it. So, let's close this chapter with a look at how to make good decisions about your web content.

INVOLVE THE RIGHT PEOPLE

If you are a media property, then you probably have this figured out. If you're not a media property, take inspiration from one. You need someone, such as an editor-in-chief (or use whatever title you like), and supporting staff. (For a detailed explanation of roles, see Kristina Halvorson's *Content Strategy for the Web.*) That team should act as content stewards, with input from important stakeholders such as sales, marketing, and subject matter experts (SMEs). Trust that team to call the shots about web content. The final call should come from the editor-in-chief.

Avoid SME Syndrome (But Don't Avoid SMEs)

SMEs, such as scientists or engineers, are experts in their subject matter. They're not experts in content, communication, editing, or writing. So, SMEs should help assess whether content presents a topic or product accurately. SMEs should *not* make the final call about web content.

When SMEs have too much control over the content, it becomes too detailed, unclear, and sometimes pompous. That's what I call SME Syndrome. When SMEs have too little input, big mistakes can happen. So, the tension between being accurate and being influential is healthy. An editor-in-chief or content strategist handles that tension well.

For example, while writing this chapter, a new client called me asking for help with a dispute between scientists and marketers over a URL. The scientists wanted a very scientific name, such as "nonpharmaceutical interventions." The marketers wanted a friendlier name, such as "stop germs." After a few minutes of talking through the situation—especially the users the client wanted to reach—the relieved client said, "I knew you were the right person to get this resolved!" That's what an editor or content strategy role can do for you.

USE THE RIGHT CRITERIA AND AMOUNT OF TIME

Your efforts to plan content create a useful framework for decisions. Your style guide, editorial calendar, and understanding of ethics (see Chapter 11), for example, will make day-to-day decisions easier and more efficient.

Take more time thinking through and discussing less typical decisions, such as dealing with a crisis, telling a complicated story, responding to an unexpected result, or trying a new approach.

ADMIT AND CORRECT WRONG DECISIONS

Even with all the right safeguards in place, a mistake will happen occasionally. To preserve your credibility, it's best to admit and correct the mistake as soon as possible. For example, media properties will publish errata (a fancy word for corrections) at the end of an original article. If the mistake pertains to using or buying your product or service, you might need to notify customers in other ways, such as directly through email. (For tips, see the *Consumer Reports* guidelines in Chapter 4.)

SUMMARY

Evaluate your web content to assess your progress toward clout. As you evaluate, decide when and how to change course. With time, you will reach the top of this higher and harder road—and earn a weighty responsibility. Learn more about ethics in Chapter 11.

REFERENCES

1   The Day 2 Problem: A Tour of Editorial Strategy with Jeffrey MacIntyre at http://blip.tv/file/3292757

2   Colleen Jones, Kevin O'Connor, Testing Content: Early, Often, and Well at http://www.slideshare.net/leenjones/content-testing-early-often-well

11 REACH THE TOP— BUT DON'T STOP

· ·

When your web content influences the results you want, you've achieved clout. But, your journey doesn't end there. Influence brings much responsibility at a time when ethics are fuzzy. And, the future of technology is quickly becoming now. Will you and your web content be ready?

WE HAVE TO BE ABLE TO CRITICIZE WHAT WE LOVE, TO SAY
WHAT WE HAVE TO SAY, 'CAUSE IF YOU'RE NOT TRYING TO MAKE
SOMETHING BETTER, THEN...YOU ARE JUST IN THE WAY.

—Ani DiFranco, musician and songwriter

You've climbed the higher and harder way to influence results, but you haven't reached the end of the road. It's more like the first peak in a long mountain range. As you earn clout, you face ethical responsibilities and astounding opportunities.

USE CLOUT RESPONSIBLY OR LOSE IT

When you have influence or pull, you attract the users you want to attract, and they're likely to give you some slack if you make a mistake. When users trust you to influence them, you have a tremendous responsibility to them.

RESPONSIBILITY STARTS WITH THE TRUTH

The more clout you have, often the less you have to prove your credibility or provide lots of evidence. Why? Because users assume you're continuing the due diligence that earned you clout in the first place (**Figure 11.1**). That puts the burden *on you* to ensure that what you say is accurate and based in reality. Will your brand, idea, product, or service really deliver what your web content promises and supports? Are you helping users make good decisions that are not only in your best interests but also in theirs? If not, you risk violating your users' trust in a big way.

Figure 11.1: As your clout grows, users look for less evidence of your credibility and claims, which may tempt you to cut corners.

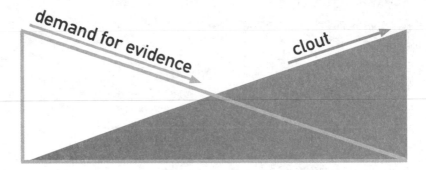

Now, even if you're doing your due diligence to ground your content efforts in the truth, you need to consider ethics. An ethical fog has rolled into our industry as different perspectives on content merge. Let's shed some light on it.

OUR CONTENT ETHICS ARE MASHING UP

As we merge different content on our websites and connect our websites to social networks, we're trying to mix conflicting content perspectives and, consequently, ethics (**Figure 11.2**).

Figure 11.2: Different ethical perspectives are colliding.

Publishing: Content Is a Copyrighted Asset

A publisher or media property such as HowStuffWorks.com expends much time, effort, and money to create quality web content that attracts the right users, or audiences, and is supported by advertising or subscriptions. The content is a valuable, copyrighted asset.

Marketing/Public Relations: Content Is for Building Brand Reputation

Web content builds an organization's reputation by telling the brand story, demonstrating the brand culture, and delivering on brand promise. The reputation is the asset.

Also, as marketing becomes more closely aligned with publishing, marketing professionals will expend more and more time, effort, and money to create quality content that attracts the right users and provides an opportunity to show the value of the organization's products or services. As a result, I expect to see brands treat content more and more like a publisher does— like a valuable asset.

Social Networking/Media: Content Is for Building Relationships

For social networking, sharing web content is a way to build relationships or a community. The content is less important than the relationships with users. The relationships are the asset.

This perspective can be good. When people share a link to web content with their social networks, they promote (or distribute) it to users who are likely to be interested in it. That's a win-win situation.

This perspective can also be bad. For example, if a blogger republishes an entire article by HowStuffWorks.com without permission in the name of sharing it, he takes website traffic and advertising revenue away from the article's source. He also violates the licensing terms of the photos in the article. If he has advertising on his own blog, he reaps revenue instead of HowStuffWorks.com. If he republishes the article with mistakes or with low-quality advertising, he also damages the credibility of the article and, possibly, its author and source. That's a win-lose situation.

Reputation and Relationships Are Assets That Depend on Content Assets

To start resolving the ethical conflicts, integrate these perspectives on content. Your content assets are closely connected to other assets, such as your relationships with users and your brand reputation. When you treat any of those assets carelessly, you risk ruining the value of all of them.

LET'S GET ETHICAL OR ELSE

To keep your clout, you need practical ethics now more than ever. The recommendations for credibility offered by *Consumer Reports* (see Chapter 4) and the legal considerations noted in Chapter 18 of the *Yahoo! Style Guide* (see Chapter 6) are excellent places to start. I offer these points, as well:

- Don't republish copyrighted content without permission.
- Don't hide or omit authorship and attribution.
- Don't provide form without substance, such as gibberish articles for SEO or fake quotes and case studies.
- Don't take advantage of disadvantaged users, such as offering credit cards to users who you know are already in a bad financial situation.

- Don't use users' data or otherwise intrude on their privacy without their explicit permission.

Besides responsibility, you also have new opportunities thanks to maturing technology and users' readiness to adopt it.

Against Mind Control

. . . .

I find few things more disturbing than viewing persuasion or influence as "mind control." That's exactly how some interactive designers and marketers have described it. I even watched a presentation one time comparing website users to waterskiing squirrels—easily manipulated by positive reinforcement. Users are smarter than squirrels. So, let's settle this mind control nonsense once and for all.

First, mind control is not appealing. I don't know of anyone who would like to have her mind controlled by anyone other than herself. So, what's the point in talking about mind control as a goal?

Second, mind control might not be possible at all, much less through a website. Scientists and psychologists hotly contest whether mind control even exists, and there is no diagnosis of mind control, brainwashing, neurolinguistic programming (NLP), or a similar condition recognized by the American Psychological Association (APA).

Third, the idea of mind control encourages violating users' privacy. If you seek to control minds, then it would be in your best interest to exploit every private detail about your users' thoughts and behavior. Ick.

So, let's face reality, respect users, and focus on influence—not mind control.

LOOK AHEAD TO NEW PROSPECTS

As technology brings new possibilities, you'll gain more chances to influence results through content.

LOCATION, LOCATION, LOCATION + CONTENT, CONTENT, CONTENT

Technology now allows us to know a key element of context—the user's geolocation—and respond with the right content (**Figure 11.3**).

Figure 11.3: Technology tells us more about context—literally where a user is.

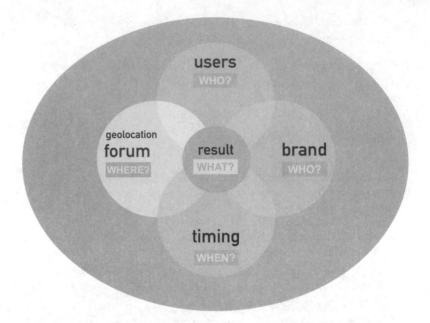

This technology is known as location-based services (LBS) and often goes hand in hand with mobile devices. It's not a stretch to imagine the value of useful, local content for theme parks, travel destinations, conferences, large stores, and even college compuses. (See the following sidebar.) As with any technology, however, don't be seduced by the features without thinking through your content.

MULTICHANNEL + MASHUPS = MORE PRESSURE FOR CONTENT STRUCTURE

In Chapter 2, I discussed the importance of content structure to quality content. Well, that importance is only going to intensify. The more structured your content is, the better you can repackage it for different channels, devices, and forums. You also can better combine it with other content or data. So, ironically, the more structured your content is, the freer it is. Rachel Lovinger, Content Strategy Lead at Razorfish, offers this perspective:

"Publishing content that's marked up with smart structure and metadata allows it to be delivered on a wider range of channels, while still retaining the context and relationships that make it meaningful and useful to

Content and Connection Drive Location-Based Services at North Carolina State University

Universities and colleges are physical and emotional communities. A campus, by its nature, creates and engenders shared experiences. This common sense of place gives a university or college a singular opportunity to create and deliver content based on geographic location.

Using essential concepts that power location-based services, North Carolina State University is exploring ways to offer location-aware content that helps build connections between people and the university.

The exploration began with pairing location and content for the Chancellor Visits website. As the newly appointed chancellor traveled across North Carolina to learn more about the university's role and to reaffirm the university's commitment to meeting the state's needs, the website plotted the visit locations on an interactive map.

Tim Jones, the university's Director of Web Communication, explains, "Each map location pointed to a dense collection of background material, photos, video coverage of the Chancellor's remarks, interviews with alumni and friends, and any other content created during the visits to each location."

Using location as the organizing principle brought new life to content that might have otherwise gone unnoticed.

"We could visualize the breadth and reach of NC State University with a simple map," says Jones. He also notes that anecdotal evidence and a steady increase in traffic to the website suggest the effort was a success.

Now, NC State is evolving its location-based efforts by piloting a university-specific service called On Campus. The service is a hyper-local mobile application that lets users check in to locations, share photos and videos from those locations, earn digital awards, redeem location-specific promotions, find campus events based on location, and connect with their friends.

On Campus also integrates other popular location-based services—including Foursquare, Gowalla, and Facebook—allowing users to check in and connect to friends from a single tool specific to NC State. The service aggregates friends lists from these services into a single list.

"It's more important to be able to find and connect with your friends than it is to know what service your friends use to check in," notes Jones.

Knowing where their users are gives NC State additional context—type of location, typical interactions that take place in the location, distinct knowledge of the physical environment—that informs the content offered.

As Jones explains, "If a user checks in to a dining hall, we can provide a mobile-friendly menu, nutritional information, and recommendations for side items. And this is just the start. Our hope is that we can use our location-based services to influence interactions in both digital and physical spaces."

both your audience and your brand. Think of it like providing publishing instructions with the content, where each different platform uses only the instructions that are relevant."

MAKE THE MOST OF THESE OPPORTUNE MOMENTS

I can't end this book without extending a special call to two industries.

HEALTH INDUSTRY, IT'S TIME TO CATCH UP

The health industry has quality content resources such as MayoClinic.com, WebMD.com, and CDC.gov. But, there's much more that web content can do to help patients and health practitioners make good decisions.

Medical and Personal Health

Imagine having access to the right combination of content and data to help

- Patients make healthy everyday choices and manage appointments.
- Patients cope with chronic disease including appointments, prescriptions, and connecting with other patients.
- Clinicians prevent, diagnose, and treat problems more accurately and efficiently.
- Clinicians better communicate with each other and with other parties in the health system, such as insurance companies and pharmacists.

Then, picture pooling the data for research to better identify symptoms and refine treatments. In *The Decision Tree: Taking Control of Your Health in the New Era of Personalized Medicine*, Thomas Goetz, the executive editor of *Wired*, outlines the possibilities and offers early examples. We need those possibilities to become a more widespread reality.

While Goetz credits technology with these possibilities, I see content strategists as critical to bringing the possibilities to life. Content strategists will help plan rules and requirements for different users and create appropriate content that helps users think and act well. Content strategists also can help structure the content so it can be reused and repackaged across different devices.

Web Content Helps Patients and Doctors Make Better Decisions

* *

Wired offers a fascinating article about web content and technology in health.[1] For example, Jeff Livingston, an obstetrician and gynecologist, explains how using web content helps him better collaborate with patients on diagnoses and treatments.

" 'If you think about the way you go to a doctor, it's kind of upside down. In a ten-minute visit, six or seven minutes are spent gathering background information ... Then we do a quick exam and run a test, and then spend the last few seconds talking about what we're going to do,' Livingston said.

"For example, on a typical day, Livingston often has young patients asking about birth control. If they've never explored the issue, then Livingston typically spends most of his time explaining options, along with their risks and benefits. If, however, he can point his patients to online resources, such as a podcast he created and links to on Facebook, then the majority of patients already know what they want when they arrive in the office.

"What's really fascinating is how often the educated patient makes the exact same decision that I would have for them,' he said."

For more examples, see the *Wired* article "E-Health and Web 2.0: The Doctor Will Tweet You Now."

Public Health

The public health system in the United States collects and analyzes an enormous amount of data with potential for many insights. Much of that data lies dormant in a myriad of databases and applications. While the public health system gets ample funding for research, the funding to turn data into actionable insights and useful web content for health professionals and the public is comparatively slim. Frankly, I'm amazed at how much federal and state agencies have been able to do with so little. With more resources for communication and content strategy, the public health system could make the most of its data and content.

Content Strategists Will Help Get Electronic Health Records Right

. . . .

I'm ecstatic about electronic health records. They have potential to be Mint.com for our health, if not better. What are they? They're the organized digital version of that messy, overstuffed paper file at your doctor's office. Personal electronic health records help us track our own health and communicate efficiently with doctors and hospitals. They also help doctors and other clinicians communicate efficiently with each other about you, with your permission. No more delays because one doctor's office forgets to fax part of your record to another doctor's office.

For electronic health records to reach their potential, content strategists must be involved in planning and defining them. Content strategists have expertise in planning what content a user should see when and how best to support a user's decision.

A Special Note About Mental Health and Social Work

For mental health and social work, the possibilities are similar to those for medical and public health. But, the likelihood of turning those possibilities into reality is grim right now. My husband has worked as a licensed clinical social worker and therapist for more than 10 years. He also has his Ph.D. focused on program evaluation, or researching whether a treatment program works. He has to advocate constantly for better use of technology, data, and content. The right combination of technology, data, and content would do wonders for day-to-day logistics, managing cases across the social work system, communicating with multiple families, and conducting long-term research to evaluate which programs work and which ones don't.

It's hard to express the level of ignorance about and lack of resources for technology, data, and content in this realm. I wouldn't believe it unless I heard the stories daily. But, the potential is great. The return on investment from improved productivity in case management alone likely would justify much of the costs. To find out—and to avoid being left completely behind—the fields of mental health and social work need more awareness of, expertise in, and resources for technology, data, and content.

INTERACTIVE, LET'S FULFILL OUR PROMISE

Remember the bubble that burst in 2000? (Yeah, I try to forget it, too.) The interactive industry has the opportunity to redeem itself now. I haven't spent my entire career here to watch it be belittled by snake oil, overpromised technology, design without substance, or inappropriate marketing and advertising. I've spent my career here because I, like many people, want to change things for the better. The interactive industry has a unique opportunity to help users make the best decisions they can and to help clients or stakeholders get results. The stars have aligned—enough people are using websites, technology is ready, and there's more appreciation for design and content strategy now than ever. We're *almost* in perfect position.

What would make our position perfect? More clout with our clients and stakeholders. It's time to grow up. I don't mean we can't have fun. But, we can't treat the opportunity that lies ahead lightly. We have to be trusted advisors. As Seth Godin and Don Peppers explain

"Corporations pay consultants billions of dollars for their advice.... Why the premium? Because Bain and McKinsey and the like are trusted advisors. They've built enough of a track record, and enough confidence, that they can command a substantial premium."[2]

Being a trusted advisor sometimes means saying what our clients *need* to hear, not what they *want* to hear. Even though the road to influential web content is hard, it's the right road for lasting results. So, let's roll up our sleeves and lead our clients and stakeholders on their journey to clout.

SUMMARY

During the climb to clout you plan, evaluate, and adjust your influential web content. You overcome roadblocks along the way. When you reach the top, enjoy the results. But, remember you're not at the end of the road. You face more ethical responsibility—and more opportunity. The same principles and tenacity that helped you reach new heights with new results will keep you there.

REFERENCES

1   *Wired*. Ehealth and Web 2.0: The Doctor Will Tweet You Now at http://www.wired.com/epicenter/2010/05/e-health-and-web-20-the-doctor-will-tweet-you-now/2/

2   Seth Godin and Don Peppers, *Permission Marketing: Turning Strangers into Friends and Friends into Customers* (Simon and Schuster, 1999)

RECOMMENDED READING

The following books and online publications should prove helpful in your efforts to create influential web content.

BOOKS

Argumentation: The Study of Effective Reasoning (David Zarefsky)

Audience, Relevance, and Search (James Mathewson, Frank Donatone, Cynthia Fishel)

Brandraising (Sarah Durham)

BrandSimple (Allen P. Adamson, Sir Martin Sorrell)

Card Sorting (Donna Spencer)

Click: What Millions of People Are Doing Online and Why It Matters (Bill Tancer)

Communicating Design (Dan Brown)

Content Management Bible (Bob Boiko)

Content Strategy for the Web (Kristina Halvorson)

The Decision Tree: Taking Control of Your Health in the New Era of Personalized Medicine (Thomas Goetz)

Designing Brand Identity (Alina Wheeler)

Engage (Brian Solis)

Everything's an Argument (Andrea A. Lunsford, John J. Ruszkiewicz)

How We Decide (Jonah Lehrer)

Letting Go of the Words (Ginny Redish)

Marketing Metaphoria (Gerald Zaltman, Lindsay Zaltman)

Marketing: Unmasked (Erik Wolf, Stephanie Frost)

Mental Models (Indi Young)

Neuro Web Design (Susan M. Weinschenk)

Nudge: Improving Decisions About Health, Wealth, and Happiness (Richard H. Thaler, Cass R. Sunstein)

Observing the User Expereience (Mike Kuniavsky)

Remote Research (Nate Bolt, Tony Tulathimutte)

Search Analytics (Louis Rosenfeld, Marko Hurst)

Strategic Market Research (Anne Beall)

Sway: The Irresistible Pull of Irrational Behavior (Ori Brafman, Rom Brafman)

Web Analytics 2.0 (Avinash Kaushik)

The Web Content Strategist's Bible (Richard Sheffield)

The Yahoo! Style Guide (Yahoo!)

ONLINE PUBLICATIONS

10 Tips for Testing a Content Concept by Content Science at http://content-science.com/expertise/reports-tools

The Behavior Grid by BJ Fogg at http:// www.behaviorgrid.org

Consumer Reports Webwatch Guidelines at http://www.consumerwebwatch.org/consumer-reports-webwatch-guidelines.cfm

Differentiating Between Blogger Relations and Sponsored Content by Chris Brogan at http://www.chrisbrogan.com/blogger-relations-vs-sponsored-content

E-Health and Web 2.0: The Doctor Will Tweet You Now by Computerworld Staff at http://www.wired.com/epicenter/2010/05/e-health-and-web-20-the-doctor-will-tweet-you-now

Exploring Editorial Strategy by Jeffrey MacIntyre at http://www.slideshare.net/Predicate/predicate-exploring-editorial-strategy-3765915

How to Put Together an Editorial Calendar for Content Marketing by Michele Linn at http://www.contentmarketinginstitute.com/2010/08/content-marketing-editorial-calendar

How Users Read on the Web Redux by Colleen Jones at http://www.leenjones.com/2009/06/how-users-read

Myth: People Read Less Online by Erin Kissane at http://incisive.nu/2010/myth-people-read-less-online

The Nimble Report by Rachel Lovinger at http:// nimble.razorfish.com

Rethinking Marketing by Roland T. Rust, Christine Moorman, and Gaurav Bhalla at http://hbr.org/2010/01/rethinking-marketing/ar/1

Toward Content Quality by Colleen Jones at http://uxmatters.com/mt/archives/2009/04/toward-content-quality.php

Who Rocks the Party? By Margot Bloomstein at http://www.slideshare.net/mbloomstein/who-rocks-the-party

The Yahoo! Style Guide at http://styleguide.yahoo.com

INDEX